THE
PAPER
ZOO

Charlotte Sleigh

THE PAPER ZOO

500 Years of Animals in Art

The British Library

For Pascal – the elephant hawk moth
For Clem – the electric eel
For Manny – the polar bear
And for Badger – a rare find indeed

First published in 2016 by
The British Library
96 Euston Road
London NW1 2DB

ISBN 978 0 7123 5743 2

Designed by Maggi Smith, Sixism
Picture research by Sally Nicholls
Printed and bound in China by C&C Offset Printing Co., Ltd

Frontispiece: '*Purple-bellied Lory
(Lorius hypoinochrous)*'.
Original watercolour, later engraved as plate 170
in George Edwards, *A Natural History of
Uncommon Birds, and of Some Other Rare
and Undescribed Animals*, London, 1743–51.

Title page: '*Chameleon forest dragon,
Lophyrus tigrinus*'. From *Bijdragen tot de
dierkunde* ('Contributions to Zoology'),
Amsterdam, first edition of journal, 1848.

This page: '*A Cheetah standing on a ground*'.
Watercolour by a Calcutta artist, *c*. 1820.
Hastings Albums (collected by the Marquess of
Hastings and Lady Hastings, Bengal, 1813–23).

Contents

Pullus pipit, das Küchlein pipet/	pi pi	P p
Cuculus cúculat, der Kukuck kucket/	kuk ku	Q q
Canis ringitur, der Hund marret/	err	R r
Serpens sibilat, die Schlange zischet/	si	S s
Graculus clamat, der Heher schreyet/	tae tae	T t
Bubo ululat, die Eule uhuhet/	ú ú	U u
Lepus vagit, der Hase quäcket/	vá	W w
Rana coaxat, der Frosch quacket/	coax	X x
Asinus rudit, der Esel ygaet/	y y y	Y y
Tabanus dicit, die Breme summet/	ds ds	Z z

Introduction

Angus the Antelope lives in Angola.

Many are the long journeys that have been passed by playing some variant of this game. The rules vary from one tradition to another, but they generally involve a progression through the alphabet with prescribed nouns of various kinds. Each player takes it in turn to elaborate on successive letters.

Betty the Bison lives in Barnsley.

Although it can be played with foods, or cars, or anything else, animals are somehow always the first choice. There is a particular pleasure in constructing a complete set of animals which maps onto a finite framework of language, neatly bounded by the edges of the alphabet.

The Moravian Johann Amos Comenius (1592–1670) was almost certainly the first to link animals with the alphabet. His *Orbis sensualium pictus* ('The Visible World in Pictures') related different phonemes to animal noises, in order to make letters easier – and certainly more fun – to memorise. Animals were also prominent in other early children's didactic literature; learning to read and learning to identify animals were apparently adjacent skills. Animal alphabets in their modern form emerged around 1800; Thomas Bewick's *A General History of Quadrupeds* (1790) ran from Adive, a jackal, to Zorilla, a kind of skunk.

A different kind of animal set that has been historically much loved by children is Noah's Ark. Just as A and Z constrain and complete the linguistic animal collection, so the gopher-wood confines of Noah's vessel enclose the fullness of God's Creation. A child's toy recreates the sense of completeness; although it cannot contain two of *everything*, the sense of comprehensiveness when all the fauna are safely aboard is just the same. Two of every kind: the set is complete. It is a box from which Creation can be remade afresh.

And indeed, for thinkers and writers of the late Renaissance, Noah's Ark was a powerful stimulus to natural research, setting a standard and a form for animal collection. For the Italian natural philosopher Ulisse Aldrovandi (1522–1605) the creation of a museum was a pious endeavour worthy of the patriarch; it should contain all of God's Creation, and be ordered according to the divine plan. Aldrovandi assembled a vast collection of specimens – both zoological and botanical – and set them out in his studio. He was rewarded by having the papal legate say that his was indeed 'the work of another Noah'.[1]

Hand-coloured alphabet page (P–Z) from Johann Amos Comenius, *Orbis sensualium pictus*, Nuremberg, 1659

Comenius' book, first published in German and Latin, is commonly regarded as the first picture book for children. It taught letters onomatopoeically, with the owl's call rendered 'u' and the buzzing of a fly 'z'. This connection between language and the animal kingdom was to run as a theme through history. Later chapters discussed the natural history of animals, as well as humankind and the deity.

The three decks of Noah's Ark.
Athanasius Kircher, *Arca Noë*,
Amsterdam, 1675

Kircher's learning was both extraordinary and bizarre. Here, he attempts to recreate the likely layout of Noah's Ark. In other works Kircher attempted to translate birdsong into musical notation, suggesting a universal language based upon melody rather than the spoken word. Being related to mathematics, music was possibly the language of God, used to speak the animals into life.

However, repeating the work of Noah seemed an increasingly unattainable goal as the years passed. Discoveries that were shipped back from the New World constantly added to the sum of ancient knowledge, which until then had been assumed to be correct and complete. It was perhaps for this reason that the polymath Athanasius Kircher (1602–1680) so obsessively analysed the achievements of Noah in the light of modern knowledge, in his three-volume *Arca Noë* ('Noah's Ark', 1675). Kircher counted the species then known to be in existence, and computed the size of the ark from biblical description: space, he concluded with relief, was there enough for all – even including the additional specimens necessary for the sustenance of the carnivores.

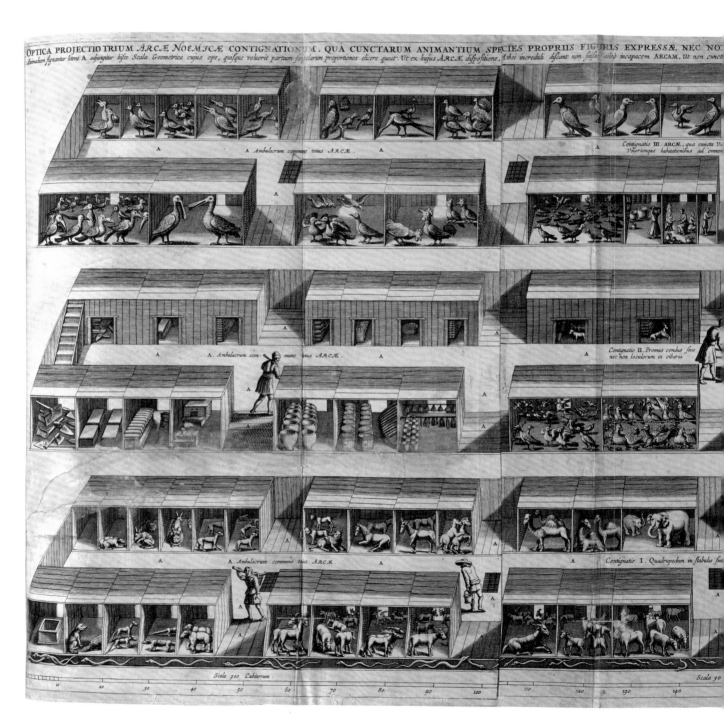

Around 1625, twenty years after Aldrovandi's death, Cassiano dal Pozzo (1588–1657) took a different approach, and instead of assembling an unmanageably large physical collection, began to create a 'paper museum', as he dubbed it. This was, unusually for its day, a collection of drawings and paintings of objects from contemporary natural history, as well as from antiquity.[2] Cassiano was partly making a virtue of necessity, for though wealthy he was not in the same patronage league as Aldrovandi and could not perhaps afford such grand-scale ventures in physical collection. But he was also responding to new ventures in drawing the natural world, being excited and intrigued by the possibilities of visual knowledge.

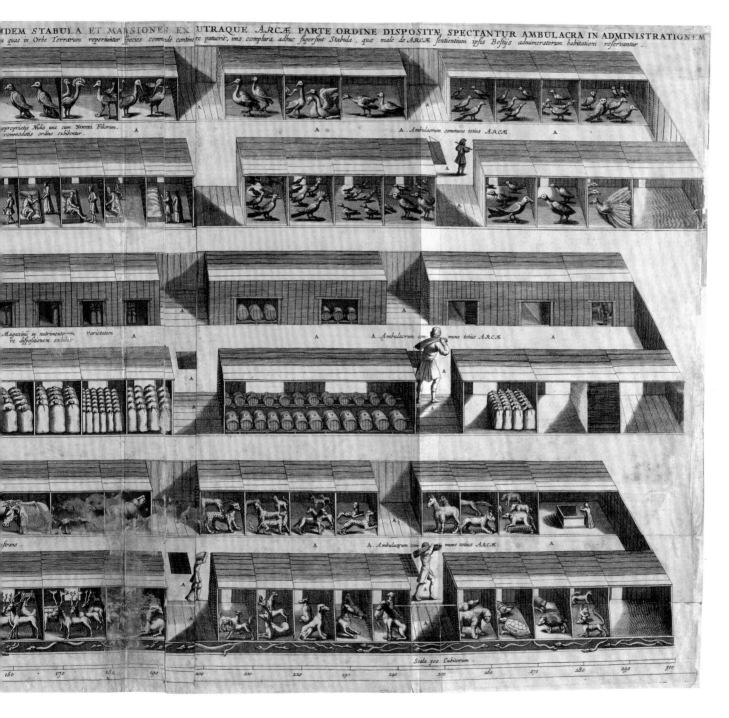

Collecting live animals was even more difficult, dangerous, and expensive than amassing dead specimens. For many centuries, only royalty could boast of menageries, and only their invited guests could see them. The zoological gardens, or zoo, was an innovation of the early nineteenth century. It drew the middle and eventually the working classes into a new relationship with animals; animals were a form of entertainment that was intended to be educational, respectable, and rational. For the Victorians, zoos were just one example of a fashion for panoramas. Like the Great Exhibition of 1851, zoos gave an overview of the world in its entirety. One could return home from a visit, foot-weary but content that one had seen all that there was to be seen. Although the zoo was not established until relatively recently in history, we can productively treat collections of animal images – whether as a loose-leafed portfolio or within a printed book – as fulfilling many of the functions and satisfactions of those real animal collections. Animal pictures were, in their earliest days, expensive in their own right, but they were nevertheless more affordable than the real thing: a democratised menagerie. They became increasingly so. Even today, wallcharts, spotter's guides, and the like fulfil a similar ambition, representing a world completely surveyed and overseen.

Yet theirs is a sense of completeness that can only be maintained by turning a blind eye to the evidence. Whereas early naturalists could legitimately hope for a taxonomy of divine order, today we are faced with unplanned diversity. Modern science uncovers the breadth of variation, shows us the fuzziness of species boundaries, and gestures at the extent of what we do not know. Even so, the compulsion to collect and complete remains, and the paper zoo fulfils it in a way that a material zoo never can.

By opening the covers of a book, the reader enters through the gates of the paper zoo.

Choosing to draw: philosophy and aesthetics

Whatever else the Romans may have done for us, teaching us to draw was not one of their gifts. Aldrovandi complained wistfully: 'one cannot imagine anything more useful; if the ancients had drawn and painted all of the things which they described, one would not find so many doubts and endless errors among writers'.[3] The two great works of classical scholarship on animals were Aristotle's *History of Animals*, and Pliny the Elder's *Naturalis historia* ('Natural History', 77–79 ce); this contained commentary on other features of nature besides). Neither Pliny nor his Greek predecessor included any illustrations in their natural histories. Everything was done by words.

Instead, animals began to appear in medieval works of art. In glass, they were biblical symbols: the Lamb of God; or the lion, ox, and eagle that represent three of the evangelists. Manuscripts, too, contained such pious beasts, but often also more vivacious animals: monkeys capering around the edges of the text, or snails creeping through its borders. Books devoted to animals – bestiaries – were a combination of piety and entertainment. The behaviours of animals gave moral lessons to readers; the hoopoe, for example, was renowned for caring for its parents, licking the mist from their eyes in fulfilment of the fifth commandment (honour thy father and mother). Such moral lessons were juxtaposed with altogether juicier titbits; the hoopoe was also a filthy bird, eating and constructing its nest from human excrement; its blood, if smeared on a sleeping man, would attract devils to come and strangle him. These facts were most often recycled from Pliny, who had himself got them from folklore from around the Roman world. The hoopoe's unappealing qualities did not, it seems, in any way diminish its moral–pedagogical relevance, nor pagan tales conflict with orthodox theology. The illustrated animal was above all an emblem, the representation of some divine or virtuous quality.

However, for some, pictures were problematic. St Bernard of Clairvoux, writing in the early twelfth century, expressed anxiety about the power of the visual image to distract from God's Word:

> But in the cloister, under the eyes of the Brethren who read there, … to what purpose are those unclean apes, those fierce lions, those monstrous centaurs, those half-men, those striped tigers[?] … [S]o many and so marvellous are the varieties of divers shapes on every hand, that we are more tempted to read in the marble than in our books, and to spend the whole day in wondering at these things rather than meditating the law of God. For God's sake, if men are not ashamed of these follies, why at least do they not shrink from the expense?[4]

But St Bernard was in the minority. Bestiaries continued to be produced and collected through the late medieval period, and their animal images proliferated in gargoyles, on church pillars and misericords, on tapestries and maps and coats of arms. Meanwhile other manuscripts and incunabula (printed matter from before 1500) collected knowledge of the natural world more broadly. These were writings on the 'book of nature', that is, the created world considered as a complement to the book of revelation – the Bible – as an exposition of God's order. A few wealthy patrons and manuscript-owners commissioned artists to add illustrations to their copies of these authoritative, but officially picture-free, natural-historical texts. A 1481 incunabulum of Pliny's *Naturalis historia*, for example, was annotated over the next few decades by its owner, with additional marginal illustrations commissioned by the author of the notes. These include a handful of mammals and birds, but

Opening showing lion, leopard, hare and elephant, from a North Italian bestiary and herbal manuscript, Lombardy, *c.* 1440

Medieval bestiaries were not intended to be natural histories in anything like a modern, scientific sense. Nevertheless, it is difficult not to be amused at the elephant in this drawing, perhaps the artist's incredulous response to a second- or third-hand description.

predominant among the animals – by a long way – are aquatic species. Moreover, the drawings of these creatures – unlike the schematic and conventional images of land-dwellers – have a level of observational portraiture that sets them apart from their marginal neighbours, with shadowing and tattered fins which suggest that their models must have lain on the artist's table.[5]

Albrecht Dürer (1471–1528) was the earliest Northern European to theorise drawing. Taking his cue from the Roman architect Vitruvius, he tried to give ideal proportions for rendering the human body in pictorial form, but found he could not. Forced to conclude that beauty was substantially in the eye of the beholder, he instead advised his readers simply to draw what they saw:

> The life that is in nature reveals the truth of these things. Therefore look closely at it, take it as your guide, and do not depart from nature in what seems good to you, by believing that your own instinct is better, for that will lead you astray. For truly: art is rooted in nature, if you can draw it out then it will be yours.[6]

Emerging from a Renaissance set of questions about the human form and portraiture, Dürer's drawings of a beetle and a hare, to name but two, set a benchmark for the emergent Northern European standard of art that was made (to use the Dutch term) *naer het leven*, or 'from the life'. In German, this truthfulness of images was designated by the term *nach dem Leben*. The term had been in use for some decades as a guarantee of natural-historical accuracy before it was incorporated more generally into a theory of aesthetics, a standard for all art, in Karel van Mander's *Schilder-Boeck* ('The Book of Painters', 1604).[7] Lifelike aesthetics provoked philosophical questions about how the mind saw and remembered visual things. Alongside the development of the 'from the life' method, artists – Dürer and Leonardo da Vinci, to name two – also drew new models of the brain to explain and affirm its combination of imaginative and documentary faculties.

Around the same time a second set of phrases emerged: *ad vivum*, *au vif*, and *al vivo*, which have sometimes been conflated with the terms used by Dürer and his ilk, but have a subtly different meaning – an inclination of the image *towards* life, rather than somehow produced from it. It was most particularly in botany that the standard had value; pressed flowers were considered by some to be the very definition of an *ad vivum* image.[8] An image could stand in for a specimen for the purposes of description and identification. Even a drawing could be substituted for a specimen that would fade, wilt, or crumble when sent from one city to another, or one continent to another. With the exception of butterflies and some other insects, such tricks were not available to those interested in animals. Nor, perhaps, were the standard descriptive categories for animals so well worked out: there were no easy equivalents for number of petals, shape of leaves, and so on. Nevertheless, the broad ambition of producing an image that was 'true to life' was applied to all kinds of drawing, both plant and animal, with varying types – and varying degrees of precision – of meaning.

The designation of truth-to-life almost certainly played a broader rhetorical role in the case of animal images than a simple claim of informational interchangeability with the real thing. Roelandt Savery (1576–1639) wrote it boldly on his drawings in the place where one would normally expect the artist's

Author's portrait from title page of Johannes Goedaert, *Metamorphosis et historia naturalis insectorum*, Middleburg, 1662-9

Goedaert made an important contribution to the history of animal illustration, developing a consistent visual arrangement for the stages of insect life. His pictures showed the caterpillar at the top, the pupa below it, and the adult at the bottom, thus breaking the visual convention that the most significant form should take centre-stage.

JOANNES GOEDARTIUS
Pictor Medioburgenfis.

W Eversdyck Pinx.   R. à Perfrn fculp.

De Camelo. A. Lib. I. 163

Camel. Conrad Gessner, *Historiae animalium*, Tiguri, 1551–8

The camel's exotic credentials are confirmed by the heavily moustached figure who leads it. In the picture-only version of Gessner's books, the *Icones animalium*, a one-hump dromedary was used instead, borrowed from a fifteenth-century account of a pilgrimage to the Holy Land.

signature to go. In some cases, perhaps it simply meant the early-modern equivalent of 'I woz 'ere', or at least, 'I drew this first', indicating that the artist had not made a copy of another image, a commonplace practice. In a culture that was beginning to prize rare and unique specimens, and to value first-hand, first-refusal encounters with the exotic, 'from the life' may have had a more general value. The Dutch Golden Age, which produced the aesthetics of life-drawing, was economically founded on voyages around the globe, and we might expect the aesthetics and the economics to share some deep roots. Moreover, as various historians are beginning to show, the rhetorical force of truth-to-life did not at all wipe out emblematic concerns with animals. A lifelike drawing could still contain moral or anecdotal qualities. Thus it was for the ill-fated dodos famously drawn by Savery *naer het leven*. Savery's dodos were the 'gluttons in the dark corners of his paintings, concerned with the bodily and the base'.[9]

Conrad Gessner's four-volume *Historiae animalium* ('History of the Animals', 1551–8) and its posthumous addendum on snakes (1587) was the first really substantial animal book to combine the encyclopedists' Christianised scholarship with the bestiary's focus on animals. As ever, Pliny and sundry folklore were the sources for Gessner's tales of animal vices, virtues, and recipes. Horses rubbed shoulders with unicorns, turkeys with griffins. Gessner's was a menagerie not just of animals, but of juxtaposed pieces of writing about them. Philology – the ancient roots of animal names – was in some ways the most important part of his account.[10] Indeed, the volume was classed by its publisher under 'grammar and rhetoric'.

Rodney the rhinoceros lives in Regensdorf

Though Gessner's written facts were not new, his pictures were. In his preface, he boldly claimed that looking at pictures was, in fact, preferable to looking at real animals:

Monk fish (*left*) and bishop fish (*right*). Conrad Gessner, *Historiae animalium*, Tiguri, 1551–8

Accounting for the trustworthy provenance of these curious creatures was a key concern for Gessner. The anti-Catholic implications of these clerical fish may have contributed to the Protestant Gessner's blanket ban in the Church's *Index librorum prohibitorum* ('List of Prohibited Books').

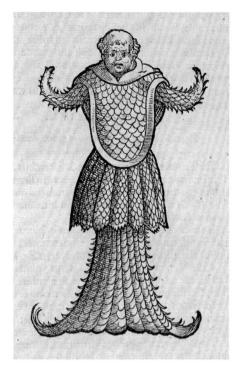

Porcupine. Edward Topsell, *The History of Four-footed Beasts and Serpents* (single-volume edition), London, 1658 (a reworking of Gessner's *Historiae animalium*)

Topsell noted that the flesh of the porcupine was 'neither very natural for meat and nourishment, nor yet very medicinable', although he did repeat Avicenna's claim that 'the powder of their quils [sic] burnt, drunk or eaten … doth promote and help conception'.

Princes of the Roman Empire used to exhibit exotic animals in order to overwhelm and conquer the minds of the populace, but those animals could be seen or inspected only for a short time while the shows lasted; in contrast, the pictures in [this book can] be seen whenever and forever, without effort or danger.[11]

Gessner is the first person on historical record to have used the pencil for drawing (previously it had been in use as a carpenter's tool). The pencil is a less demanding medium than pen and ink or watercolour; it does not require constant attention in terms of re-dipping; it does not blot. Nor, unlike charcoal, does it smudge easily if the hand travels back over areas of the paper where marks have been made. The drawings for the *Historiae* may or may not have been sketched using this new medium, but it is interesting to speculate how pencil can change the relationship between object and image. It permits an absorption in the drawn object unlike any other, such that drawing may even continue unseen, that is, without inspection of or concern with the image produced.

Gessner himself proclaimed that his images were *ad vivum*, whether drawn by himself or by his friends, but what he meant by this statement was complicated; the historian Sachiko Kusukawa concludes that it indicated the production of a reaction in the viewer identical to that produced by the original creature.[12] A drawing of a porcupine was apparently made direct from an animal shown around in Zurich by a beggar. Others were made from dried specimens, or were composite images from real, preserved parts – a toucan's beak, a hamster's pelt – and pre-existing drawings. Gessner was not above copying some pre-existing images, for example the 'Serpens maris' of Jacopo Ligozzi (page 22).[13] When Gessner was reduced to copying a picture, as he was for rare beasts, he was anxious to trace its provenance back to a reliable source. Thus, for example, he tells how a monstrous fish, with a head like a monk's, found its way into a book by Guillaume Rondelet and thence into his own. The fish was found at a specific beach in Norway, and was eventually seen by a Spanish nobleman, who commissioned a picture of it, which he gave to Queen Marguerite de Navarre, who gave it to Rondelet. The picture's validity is guaranteed by details of specific discovery, and perhaps more importantly by the character and prestige of the witnesses who created and gifted it.[14] Gessner's compunction in telling this story speaks to a historical truth which may be easily overlooked: that a picture is only as reliable as its network of production and distribution. A picture automatically tells the truth no more than a verbal tale; it must be situated in a trustworthy chain. At the first stage, there must be a respectable donor or lender of object to artist; next, the artist must have a proven track record of drawing things that could be checked against original objects. At the end of the chain there must be suitable protection from tendentious copying and pirating. Gessner's images were widely re-used for the next couple of centuries, undergoing a sort of visual Chinese Whispers

Sea-serpents.
Edward Topsell,
The History of Four-footed Beasts and Serpents
(single-volume edition),
London, 1658

Topsell's sea-serpents ran the gamut from the real to the fabulous. The 12-metre (40-foot) Baltic sea-serpents 'do never harm any man until they be provoked'; the 35-metre (120-foot) sea-serpents off the coasts of Norway were a different matter, 'very dangerous and hurtfull [sic]'. Topsell explains: '... they lift themselves above the hatches [of a ship], and suddenly catch a man in their mouths, and so draw him into the sea'.

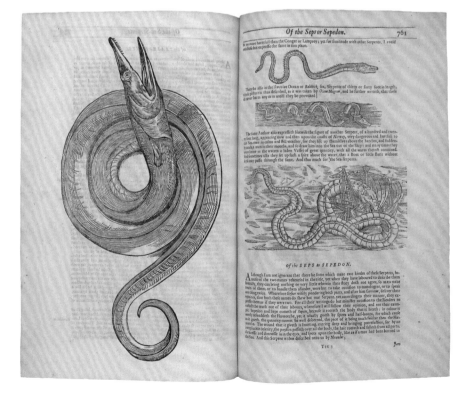

as copies were themselves copied. In Britain, Edward Topsell's *History of Four-footed Beasts* (first published 1607) was a notable example of their re-publication.

One might think that the injunction to draw true to life would sew up the list of requirements for natural-historical artists after its establishment, but a little reflection soon reveals that this was not the case. What part of an animal should be drawn? The inside or the outside? What age of animal should be shown? What stage of the life cycle? Should a perfect or imperfect specimen be chosen? Or should a generalised version be created? These different notions of objectivity have been traced painstakingly by historians, showing how idealised, perfected, corrected, typical, averaged, or characteristic forms have at various times satisfied formal desiderata.[15]

Some natural historians looked within their specimens to try to find the thing that should be pictured. In Italy the Lincei, or Academy of Lynxes (founded 1603), whose members included Galileo Galilei, did exactly this. The name of the society referred to the sharp sight commonly attributed to lynxes, and its members praised pictures as a means of representing, and holding open to scrutiny, the visual properties of nature. For example, the treatise presented by Cassiano dal Pozzo to the Academy, entitled *L'Uccelliera* ('The Aviary'), contained a Gessnerian miscellany of facts, tales, observations, and recipes, but combined these with outstanding pictures.[16] Like Aldrovandi, the Lincei aimed to impose a classical philosophical framework upon their collections, and to do this they turned to the microscope. Using this instrument, they found that the inner structures of plants lent themselves to Platonic classification based on number and symmetry. Animals were more difficult to fit into such a frame, although the microscopic studies of bees, in particular, yielded much of general philosophical interest.

In Restoration England, Robert Hooke (1635–1703) produced the most celebrated animal drawings made using a microscope. His treatise *Micrographia* (1665) is most famous for its gigantic, hunched flea, though a louse grasping a human hair runs it pretty close. *Micrographia* is naturally well known for its encomium of technically enhanced visualisation; Hooke regarded lenses as correcting the imperfections of the human senses. But interwoven with this praise of the microscope is a faith in the drawings thereby produced as guarantors of reliable knowledge. Just as lenses corrected the senses, so pictures corrected memory:

Hoopoe ('*Bubbola*') from an edition of Cassiano dal Pozzo's *L'Uccelliera*, Rome, 1622

This beautiful and euphonic bird found its medieval reputation hard to shake: 'the most nasty [species], for it eateth dung', as Cassiano's contemporary Johann Amos Comenius told his child readers.

'*The Face & Eyes of a Drone Fly*'.
Robert Hooke,
Micrographia restaurata,
London, 1745

The microscope opened up new ways of seeing animals. Many of its early adopters hoped to find God's natural order and symmetry inscribed in miniature. Later, many were to find revelations of the microbiotic and bacterial worlds – such as were contained in the River Thames – disturbing.

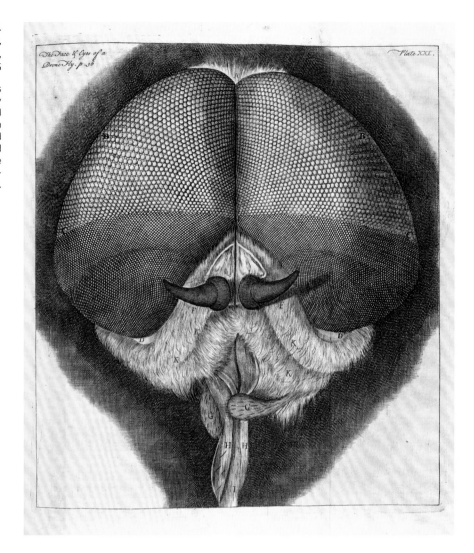

The like frailties are to be found in the Memory; we often let many things slip away from us, which deserve to be retain'd, and of those which we treasure up, a great part is either frivolous or false; and if good, and substantial, either in tract of time obliterated, or at best so overwhelmed and buried under more frothy notions, that when there is need of them, they are in vain sought for.[17]

With a book of pictures to hand, such searchings need never again be in vain.

The desire to see the insides of creatures, such as the microscope might permit, competed productively through the early modern period (the sixteenth to eighteenth centuries, approximately) with the lively trade in actual specimens: the pleasure and challenge of observing whole animals in their environments. The former practice is more usually considered natural philosophy – precursor to science – while the latter is usually counted as natural history. This is, like all taxonomies, an artificial distinction, though one that has worked reasonably well. By the nineteenth century, comparative anatomy was well established as a scientific way of studying animals, largely thanks to French practitioners. In nineteenth-century natural history, however, the gold standard of depiction was to capture the 'characteristic' appearance of birds and animals. The precise historical meaning of this adjective is hard to pin down: it seems to demand a sense of shared recognition between the artist and his or her reader. But not just any reader – shared recognition requires that the reader has almost as much experience as the artist. A characteristic image is a depiction of a creature that demands the response 'ah, yes, I recognise that; that is exactly how they are'. To the non-experienced reader, a characteristic presentation is simply a didactic device. Artist John J. Audubon's (1785–1851) birds can be read both ways. Very often, in his paintings of smaller birds at least, Audubon portrayed two or three specimens from different angles: wings spread, from above, from below, and from the side, in order to display all of their plumage. To someone unfamiliar with the birds, this was informative; to a fellow-hunter, it was characteristic.

Iceland falcon or ger falcon.
John J. Audubon,
Birds of America,
London, 1827–38

The gyrfalcon, as it is usually known today, is the largest species of the genus *Falco*, the faster-moving, beak-killing birds of prey. As is so often the case in natural history, debate revolves around its etymology, as though the name might reveal some essence of its character. Possibly it relates to 'gyre', to move in an arc – or, less poetically, to another word for 'vulture'.

Cassava plant with rustic sphinx moth
and chrysalis, and tree boa.
Maria Sybilla Merian,
*Merian dissertatio de generatione
et metamorphosibus insectorum
Surinamensium* (includes French
translation), The Hague, 1726

Although Merian followed on where
Goedaert had begun in illustrating
metamorphoses, she rejected his
schematic presentation in favour
of a synchronic depiction of all life
phases, presented upon a plant as
though simultaneously observed.

In 1812 Audubon began to draw birds on the wing, showing their shapes in flight (though this was supplemented by drawing from corpses). This was a more ambitious form of characterisation, not only because it demanded speed of drawing, but also in its demands on the reader. Such drawings depicted an essential quality that could only be recognised by familiarity in the field, never from a dead specimen. Thomas Bewick (1753–1828) was even more determined to draw from life, meaning, in his case, from the living. He made extensive use of a spyglass in order to learn the characteristic poses, movements, and comportment of wild birds; even if he could not draw them while they moved, he could judge by comparison to his mental gallery whether a drawn image looked lifelike or not. (Like Audubon, Bewick also supplemented his observations with corpses, mostly shot by his neighbour, the marvellously named aristocrat Marmaduke Tunstall).

Elements of characteristic accompanying flora were also included in many depictions, though it would be a mistake to place them uniquely in the nineteenth century. Many of them would show flowers and fruits alongside insects, for example, but these were not 'from the life' in the sense that they had been observed as such; frequently, the plants were shown at every stage from bud to fruit. In fact such presentations go back into the early modern period. For Dutch still-life painters, the inclusion of insects among fruit and flowers summoned up the ephemerality of life. For other portrayals, centred on insects, the inclusion of life stages in botanical subjects reflected a philosophical interest in metamorphosis and generation. Maria Sybilla Merian (1647–1717), for example, splayed out the developmental history of both insects and plants so that all life stages were displayed on a single, magnificent page. Claims that such-and-such an artist was the first to portray organisms in ecological context are, therefore, to be treated with caution. Often, such images remind one of nothing so much as the elegantly presented and garnished meals on food packaging, acknowledged in small print as a 'serving suggestion'.

Making drawings: techniques and reproduction

Dürer mostly produced his animal images in watercolour, and such objects, like the pictures in the collection of the Lincei, were valuable items for exchange between wealthy savants around Europe. In Restoration London, a painting of a lizard on vellum could command higher prices than portraits in oil executed by even the most fashionable painters.[18] However, reproduction was impossible; and in this sense these natural-historical images were out of line with the scientific revolution, which in so many other ways was rooted in technologies of reproduction – that is, the printing press, which despite the perils of piracy and censorship was a vital means of spreading knowledge and debate.

Instead, images were converted to woodcuts for printing. The process is one of double reverse. The original drawn image is reversed when transferred to woodblock, and re-reversed when printed back onto paper. The image cut out on the woodblock is a negative; wood is chiselled away to leave the desired lines of the drawing standing proud, ready to be inked up. It is matter of very great skill to carve

'*The Cheviot Ram*'.
Thomas Bewick,
A General History of Quadrupeds,
Newcastle upon Tyne, 1800

The image engraved here was commissioned by a breeder, anxious to record how the variety had changed over recent generations, becoming fuller and fatter through advanced practices in husbandry. By its fourth edition, the *Quadrupeds* was fully engaged in celebrating and promoting the Agricultural Revolution of the later eighteenth century.

out fine lines, and textures are not easily produced. Hence, perhaps, the curious and memorable rendering of the rhinoceros hide made by Dürer, a master of the method. Once translated to the medium of woodcut, Gessner's drawings lost their surprisingly modern appearance. The grey and coloured washes Gessner employed give a subtle sense of depth and perspective that is not retained by the strictly black and white, medieval-looking engravings. Woodcut printing is an ancient technique, but found fresh expression after the development of the printing press. Woodcuts could be set directly into the racked-up typeface of a page; they could be coated with ink and printed off at the same time as the lettering, just as many times as the page was required. Woodcuts were standard for sixteenth-century books about nature and natural philosophy.[19] Towards the very end of the eighteenth century, Thomas Bewick revived the use of woodcuts in making printed images. Using tools designed for engraving metal plates, he worked on hard wood to create robust and long-lasting cuts, which unlike copper engravings (see below) could be integrated with the printing of the text. They made the production of a whole book simpler and therefore cheaper. The wood did not deteriorate appreciably faster than the metal typeface, and cuts were often conserved and re-used.

Between the seventeenth and nineteenth century, copper engravings dominated as a medium of reproduction for natural history. Paper-printed engravings had been developed around the mid-fifteenth century, exactly when the urge for 'true-to-life' images came to the fore, and a little before illustrated books of natural history. The technique originated in Northern Europe, spread to Italy in the early Renaissance, and was reinvigorated in Northern Europe by Dürer. A very early example of its use in natural history is in Ippolito Salviani's *Aquatilium animalium historiae* ('History of Aquatic Animals', 1554). Engraving was often used as a way of copying and disseminating paintings, making a suggestive historical connection between the things that were valued enough to be reproduced in this slow and expensive way, and the cultural work that they performed. The connection with 'true-to-life' depiction was not at all intrinsic to the technique; Theodor de Bry (1528–1598) used engraving for his exotic natural histories, although he never visited the lands and fauna depicted for himself.

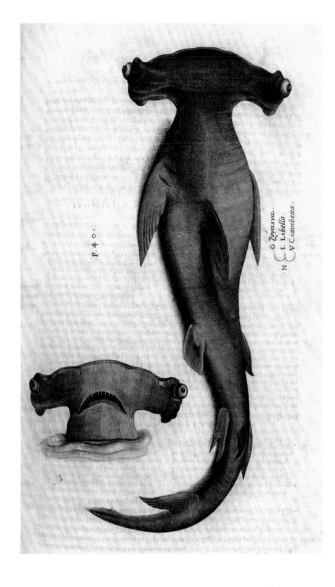

Hammerhead shark.
Ippolito Salviani,
Aquatilium animalium historiae,
Rome, 1554

This illustration is noteworthy for
including both an 'on-the-table' image
and one in which the shark pops its
head above the water, as though made
on the spot via a lightning sketch.

Engravings are made the opposite way round from wood-cuts. Instead of carving away the background to leave the lines standing proud, a smooth sheet of copper is etched to create grooves in which the ink will pool. The picture cannot be conceptualised with blocks of darkness; the whole thing must be thought of as lines, even the shadows. In wood the thickness of the lines is determined directly by the thickness of the wood ridge that is left standing proud. With engravings it is more complicated. All the cuts are of equal width, but a shallow scratch will hold little ink and print a narrow line, while a deeper one will hold more ink and print wider. The engraver must be able to judge the relationship between depth and thickness, since it will not be visible to the eye on the metal plate. The force required to score hard metal is very considerable, making these finely judged variations all the more remarkable – not to mention the control of the line itself. After the lines have been scored and the plate inked, the plate is cleaned by wiping so that all the unscored surface is free of ink. Ink only remains in the scored grooves. The paper is dampened slightly before being pressed onto the plate, so that it relaxes into the groove and, in the phrase of one commentator, 'kisses' the ink.[20] Unlike woodcuts, engravings eventually deteriorate, and the shallower the scores, the quicker this occurs. A drypoint (shallow) engraving can only be used about twenty times. Copper engraving allows for much finer-grained drawing than a woodcut, but must be printed separately from text, and collated into the finished volume. It is, for all these reasons and more (not least the cost of the materials) more expensive.

A third technique is etching, whose use in paper prints was almost contemporary with that of engraving. This is also made using a copper plate, but is much quicker and easier than engraving. The plate is first coated with a thin layer of wax, and after this has dried the artist scrapes away lines using a needle just as if he or she were making a line drawing. Compared to the act of gouging out wood or metal, the task is physically unchallenging. When the drawing is finished, the plate is placed in an acid bath. The acid eats into the exposed metal, unprotected by wax – that is, where the lines have been scraped. Bubbles form in the grooves, and these too protect the metal; they are gently tickled away with a feather. After the lines have been eaten into by the acid, the plate is removed from the bath and the wax cleaned off. The lines in the metal are now ready to ink as in the process of engraving. Although the technique is apparently simple and quick, it was not always favoured. Dürer, for example, seems only to have made a handful of etchings in his lifetime. Perhaps he did not like the way that etching did not allow for lines of different thickness, although this could be achieved by a multi-stage process of re-waxing and re-dipping. Perhaps he did not like the unavoidable phenomenon of 'foul-biting', where the acid eats through the wax to create unwanted blotches in the finished product. Perhaps he had simply got used to the other methods, actively relishing the cognitive challenge of thinking back-to-front, or the physical trial of scoring up uncompromising metal.

The artist and the engraver – whether working in wood or metal – were not always the same person. An engraver would be tasked with rendering an original watercolour or line drawing as a printable image. Artists often complained that this was done unsatisfactorily:

... by doing them myself, I have retained in the prints some perfection, which would have been wanting, had I given my original draughts to engravers to copy; for they often, through want of a just understanding of the meaning of those who gave them first draughts, go a little from the author's designs, and will take some little bend and turns of strokes for the lapse of a pencil, which they will, as they purpose, correct; which sometimes robs a figure of what the author designed as its chief distinguishing mark ...[21]

The problem was compounded when worn-out metal sheets were re-engraved for further printing, coarsening the lines as they were deepened. Sometimes completely fresh elements were added, or existing ones 'corrected', according to the opinion of the engraver.

This re-usability of plates – a faint prefiguration of today's electronic copy-and-paste – had some profound effects in terms of the value imputed to images and their vehicles of publication. The visual ability to portray animals – or any other aspect of nature – competed with the other skills that were valued in natural philosophy: the power to describe, to write, to experiment, to argue in words. At different times, and in different contexts, image and text were differently placed in a hierarchy of value. Aldrovandi, that early exponent of visual resources, had his pictures made by others, notably Jacopo Ligozzi. (Ligozzi had previously been patronised by the court of the Habsburgs; he had displayed pictures of animals and plants, perhaps indicating a market for animal pictures independent of physical cabinets.) Aldrovandi praised the 'utility to students' of images, but did not see them as an art form in the elevated sense.[22]

In short, the re-usability of plates made possible a separation of artist and author. Artists are not always acknowledged – and there is even more rarely a sound grasp of the different roles played by drawers, engravers, and colourists. The many beautiful images – mostly of birds – produced by 'John' Gould (1804–1881) are often, in fact, by Elizabeth Gould, his wife (1804–1841), and after her death by several others including Edward Lear and Joseph Wolf.

All of these techniques (woodcut, engraving, and etching) reproduced pictures in black and white, but wealthy customers purchased books or pictures that had been finished by hand in watercolour. The practice goes back to Gessner and indeed some of his prints – such as those of types of weasel – are identical without this final stage of post-production. Colour was not mechanically reproducible until the later nineteenth century, and not cheaply so until the twentieth; the role of quick, reliable hand-painting thus remained essential. And yet colourists were nearly always unacknowledged contributors to a final image. They were frequently women or youngsters, and their skilled contributions are almost never recognised, even though their work generally doubled the value of a print. Through the nineteenth century and even the twentieth, what made animal books sell was the pictures, though the book was stubbornly catalogued under the name of its author.

In the eighteenth century, books began to appear that were only or primarily available in coloured form, as opposed to featuring coloration as an optional extra. Maria Sybilla

Robins ('*Erythacus rubecula*').
John Gould,
The Birds of Great Britain,
London, 1873

The bucolic and peaceful visual world of Gould's birds was intended to speak against the Darwinian doctrines of competition and selection. British fondness for the robin, now as then, allows no space for the highly aggressive behaviour of this species in the realm of popular 'fact'.

ERYTHACUS RUBECULA.

Merian's *Metamorphosis insectorum Surinamensium* ('Transformations of the Insects of Surinam', 1705) was perhaps the earliest masterpiece of coloured natural history. It showed insects in lifelike colouring, in the company of plants from their surroundings. In some of her works, Merian experimented with *trompe l'œil*, painting specimens on backgrounds that themselves curled out from the page or canvas. Thus she drew attention to the cleverness of her execution, to the paradox that the more realistic something appeared, the more artful it actually was. In this sense, Merian alluded to the function of pictures in networks of European savants and collectors, traded and exchanged as stand-ins for nature. Perhaps her use of *trompe l'œil* can be regarded as a gentle reproof to this trade, with its effacement of the role of the (sometimes female) painter. Merian travelled to Surinam with her daughter, without a male companion: an extraordinary achievement for the day.

Mark Catesby (1683[?]–1749) followed in Merian's footsteps to the New World, albeit to the northern portion of the Americas. Catesby came from a good family, well-connected and wealthy, and rather despised those who sought to make a quick profit from recently discovered lands. Nevertheless, he was obliged to such men for the production of his collected prints, raising money from them in advance by subscription. These wealthy subscribers – 155 of them in total – were a mixture of philosophers and money-makers, the latter on the lookout for precious natural commodities in the colonies.[23] For such men, botany was the main science of interest, with its promise of medicines, spices, and dyes. Subsidising the study of animals as a side activity was a price worth paying. A rich gentleman who imported plants for cultivation might, indeed, also establish an exotic menagerie on the side. The sponsorship of general natural history, through the medium of expensive prints, was a gesture of learning, cultivation, and gentlemanliness that lent a desirable patina

Wampum snake. Mark Catesby, *The Natural History of Carolina, Florida and the Bahama Islands*, London, 1731–43

The lily has been cut in half to fit on the page, while the snake coils around, bouncing off the edges. There is debate amongst historians as to whether Catesby's pairings of plant and animal are purely ornamental or whether, on occasion, they imply a scientific connection.

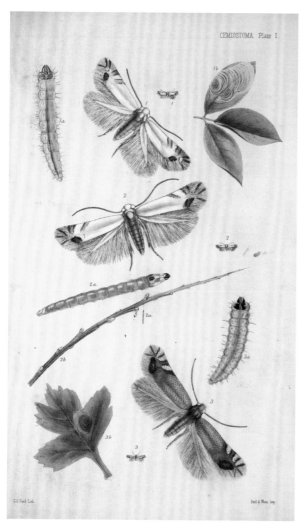

Tineid moths ('*Cemiostoma*').
H. T. Stainton,
The Natural History of the Tineina,
London, 1855–73

Surpassing the obscurity of his own thirteen volumes on British clothes moths, Henry Tibbats Stainton produced another volume on the clothes moths of Syria and Asia Minor. Perhaps in compensation for these frankly unpopular publications, he also produced an introduction to British butterflies and moths, and hosted weekly entomological soirées in his own home for interested amateurs.

to the urge to profit. Catesby's pictures came out in collections of twenty, appearing every four months. They cost a guinea apiece without colouring, or two guineas with. In relation to today's income, purchasing the coloured version equates to about £5,000 per quarter, a very significant investment in one's cultural capital.

Catesby was visually driven in his natural history, and his collections of prints were issued without text. He even taught himself to engrave, though the immediate prompt for this decision was economic; hiring a professional engraver added fatally to the cost of the project overall. (Those high prices were not purely indications of the product's status, but reflected the real costs of making it.) Catesby's engravings were made from his original watercolours, which he mostly painted in the field, employing an 'Indian' to carry his box of paints for him. Catesby had specific ideas about how best to 'serve the purpose of natural history' in making his engravings. Plants were portrayed as if flattened onto the page, and he eschewed standard patterns of hatching in favour of lines that followed the barbs and barbules of birds' feathers.[24] It has been speculated that Catesby's self-confinement to visual, as opposed to written, knowledge is responsible for his relative historical obscurity.[25] As Joyce E. Chaplin has discovered from Catesby's notes, the explorer was in fact alert to many philosophical issues of his day, and thought about them in relation to the flora and fauna he encountered. Working out how to read these intellectual traces into the pictures he produced is a big historical challenge, combined as they must have been with the aesthetic expectations of his subscribers. Like Merian, Catesby often engraved animals and birds in the same frame as plants of similar provenance. But at other times his combinations are bamboozling, most infamously his co-portrait of a flamingo and a coral. At other times, his pictures suggest the aesthetics of dissection or microscopy.

Finding subscribers to underwrite the production of a series of images was the standard way of getting animal pictures produced in the eighteenth and early nineteenth centuries. The number of copies was limited to the number of people who had engaged to buy in advance. Techniques of production were so expensive that there was no economic leverage in producing more in the hope of further sales.

Pictures of animals, once objects of individual exchange, were now part of a highly monetised system of trade. Watercolours had been unique commodities, for wealthy individuals to enjoy or to give as gifts. By the eighteenth century the medium had changed, from watercolour (in the main) to multi-copy coloured engravings – although until they were bound into books, engravings remained items for potential individual trade and collection. The medium of an animal picture determined its use, its pathways between collectors, its fate. Slowly, slowly, works such as Catesby's acquired value in the New World, not solely among wealthy collectors and traders in colonial nations of origin. Thomas Jefferson (1743–1826), a natural philosopher in his own right, was a leading figure in the project to create a truly American science. He used Catesby to demonstrate the diversity, beauty, and uniqueness of animal species in North America, in contradistinction to the claims of the prominent French naturalist, the Comte de Buffon.

After the hiatus in international trade that was caused by the Napoleonic wars, the exchange of specimens and drawings around Europe, and from further afield, exploded into life. Subsequent to this reboot, however, the market for animal images had changed. The general learned market of cultured consumers of the eighteenth century gave way to a sharper distinction between the specialist collector and the non-specialist reader. The new specialists, moreover, were not necessarily wealthy. During the nineteenth century, great series of monographs were produced on various groups within the animal kingdom, some of them impressively obscure: for example, H. T. Stainton's *Natural History of the Tineina* (clothes moths), which ran to thirteen volumes (1855–73). It was never likely to out-sell Dickens.

The new learned societies founded in the nineteenth century, composed of gentlemen of science, had the potential collectively to underwrite the cost of producing monographs that were of scientific value but had poor commercial prospects. The great new generalist society, the British Association for the Advancement of Science (founded 1831; now called the British Science Association) was approached to do just this, but declined. Its odd mixture of Cambridge dons and northern industrialists could not find common ground – at least not costly common ground – in clothes moths and the like. Instead, a smaller and more specialist collective of natural historians clubbed together to achieve the same end. Calling themselves after the celebrated English naturalist John Ray (indeed, establishing Ray as a celebrated English naturalist), they underwrote the production of unsaleable collections

Plate from John Ray's manuscript, 'A book of fishes done at Hamburgh, with Mr Ray's notes', second half of seventeenth century(?)

The appropriately named John Ray completed his friend Francis Willughby's *Historia piscium* ('Natural History of Fish', 1686). The book's publication almost brought financial ruin to its patron, the Royal Society of London.

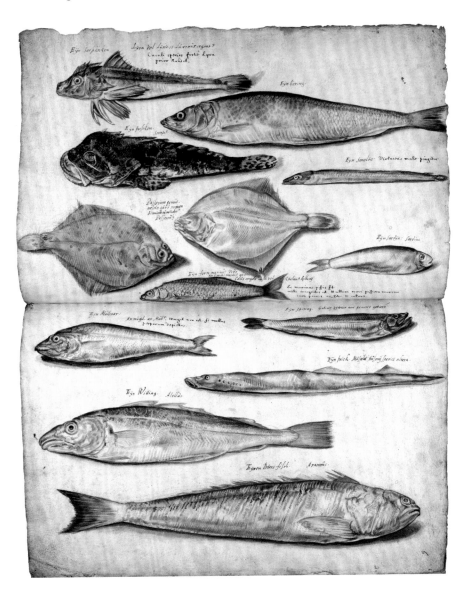

such as the four-volume *Monograph of the British Aphides* (1876–83), which cost them the equivalent of something like £100,000 in today's money: a considerable amount for a small scholarly society lacking rich patrons and well short of the 500 members initially calculated as financially necessary. The Ray Society made up in commitment what it lacked in finances, and was still in existence in the 2010s. In the nineteenth century it published Charles Darwin's more obscure works of natural history: two volumes on barnacles.

It was in this period that the most famous animal images ever created were made and sold. John J. Audubon's *Birds of America* (1827–38), of which fewer than 150 copies exist, is the most expensive modern-era publication ever sold at auction, and each surviving copy is currently worth around 12 million US dollars. Audubon, raised in France but latterly living in America, found most of his subscribers and patrons in Britain. He was a formidable entrepreneur and self-promoter. What rubbed Americans up the wrong way as boastfulness worked in his favour in England, where it came across as unvarnished, backwoods charm: his long, bear-greased hair and sweeping attire lent him a curious similarity to the magician-scientist in Joseph Wright of Derby's 1768 painting *An Experiment on a Bird in the Air Pump*. Audubon was, in many ways, the exception that proves the rule of eighteenth- and nineteenth-century natural-historical engraving. He chose his own engravers, Lizars and Havell, and with Havell in particular evolved such a mutually respectful relationship that he was able to entrust him with the completion of elements of his pictures. Moreover, Audubon did not intend to create natural-historical knowledge. His aim was to make art – which simply happened to have birds as its subject matter. In this he failed. After he died his widow sold off his paintings cheaply,

Cinnamon crabeater. William Swainson, *Zoological Illustrations*, London, 1820–3

Swainson encountered this New Zealand bird, stuffed, at an acquaintance's home in Soho, London. Swainson's pioneering use of lithography in making his illustrations was unfortunately at odds with his idiosyncratic, if not retrograde, notions of taxonomy. He abided by the quinarian system, a fivefold division of nature that extended to the angels themselves. Few were inclined to follow Swainson in his scientific ambitions.

and let the copper plates go for scrap. Audubon's pictures were dismissed as mere science, not art, for a century or more, and little valued in their country of production.[26] They were never, for example, reproduced in chromolithographic form – the common treatment of valued paintings in the late nineteenth century.

Lithography in its black and white form had been present throughout the nineteenth century, but its use was mostly restricted to cheaper, mass runs of pictures in books, rather than for expensive, collectible images. Its inked areas were neither positive, as in wood engravings, nor recessed, as in engravings. Instead the technique depends upon chemistry on a flat bed, initially limestone. Drawing with grease-based media (chalk, pencil, crayon) on the stone creates lines and areas that will attract grease-based ink, while the rest of the stone is chemically treated to repel it. Lithography overtook copper engraving as the preferred method for producing prints, as the drawing could be transferred directly onto the plate without having physically to gouge out the design. For the same reason, it was also better for rendering details, quicker, and cheaper. Many artists hated it, mostly because it was an extremely messy and laborious technique, involving acid, grease, ink, and extensive scrutiny via a magnifying glass. Edward Lear quickly gave it up as a method, but the successful publishers stuck with it. William Swainson's volumes of *Zoological Illustrations* (1820–3) were the first use of the technique in natural history, and its employment peaked with the tide of popular publications in the mid-nineteenth century.[27] Coloured printing using the same technique, or chromolithography, became widespread in the 1860s but it was expensive to set up, and only worth it for high-value books.

Specimen jars, drawers,
and natural history books.
Levinus Vincent,
Wondertoonel der nature,
Amsterdam, 1706–15

This Dutch interior demonstrates the connections between the shelving of knowledge in the form of words, and the cataloguing of knowledge embodied in real specimens. Bound engravings and framed paintings also feature in this evidently valuable collection that bridges the real, the verbal, and the pictorial.

It was many years before the camera produced images that were as aesthetically rich as those made by other media. While the photograph could betoken a tale of personal encounter, it was rarely beautiful. Animals could not be approached close enough for a good framing; they moved too fast. Small ones were hard to capture, and colours could not be reproduced at all – or only using a rather ugly form of wash over black and white halftone. The first zoological volume to use photography was an outlier, an extremely unusual endeavour in its day. This was Sylvanus Hanley's hand-coloured *The Photographic Conchology*, published in 1863. Shells, of course, stay conveniently still for the camera. The great challenge was to make images of moving creatures; the first book of wild birds using the new technique appeared in 1888. This was made possible by the happy choice of swans as subject: nice large birds which in this case were, moreover, accustomed to close human approach owing to their life on a country estate.[28]

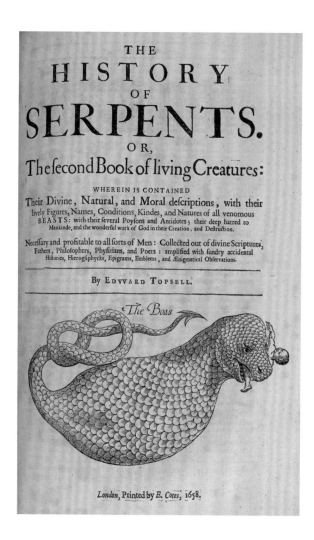

THE

HISTORY

OF

SERPENTS.

OR,

The fecond Book of living Creatures:

WHEREIN IS CONTAINED

Their Divine, Natural, and Moral defcriptions, with their lively Figures, Names, Conditions, Kindes, and Natures of all venomous BEASTS: with their feveral Poyfons and Antidotes; their deep hatred to Mankinde, and the wonderful work of God in their Creation, and Deftruction.

Neceffary and profitable to all forts of Men: Collected out of divine Scriptures, Fathers, Philofophers, Phyficians, and Poets: amplified with fundry accidental Hiftories, Hieroglihycks, Epigrams, Emblems, and Ænigmatical Obfervations.

By EDVVARD TOPSELL.

'The Boas

London, Printed by E. Cotes, 1658.

Title page,
Edward Topsell,
The History of Serpents
(Book 2 of the single-volume edition,
The History of Four-footed Beasts and Serpents), London, 1658

'Serpents' in this volume extended to insects, worms, frogs, and reptiles of many kinds. Topsell's aim was theological: to demonstrate that all creatures, even the unpleasant or traditionally demonic, were godly creations, wholesome in their bodies.

Using drawings: identification and taxonomy

A picture that stands for an animal plays a vital role in the making of knowledge. Most particularly, it plays a role in the business of priority. The first person to describe a new creature is duly recorded in the annals of natural history as its discoverer; this person, more often than not, is accorded the privilege of naming it – the privilege of Adam. Natural historians to this very day spend a great deal of time and effort clarifying the exact order in which things were described, and by whom, to find who has true priority – which is the 'real' name – and which discoveries and namings have only the status of synonym. 'Twitchers', those competitive bird-spotters much despised by ornithologists, are only different in extreme, not in kind, from the earliest specialists in the field. Although they do not name birds, they aim to be known as the first person to be accredited with a fresh and unusual sighting.

Animal specimens could not, historically speaking. be easily transported from place to place. They were too fragile, too rare, too valuable. Instead, pictures stood in for the real thing. When a naturalist found what he or she suspected to be a new species, it would be compared against the specimens that had already been painted, drawn, and reproduced. The process depended upon the completeness of the published form. Only then could a found creature be designated, potentially, as new.

Collected animal specimens also precipitated the issue of taxonomy. When a seventeenth- or eighteenth-century collector contemplated his specimens, the question of their physical arrangement immediately arose. What should go in what drawer? Which should go next to which? Historians have explored how the earliest cabinet-keepers sought to emulate Aristotle's taxonomic principles in their layouts (a tricky endeavour, given that Aristotle was not particularly concerned with taxonomy). As species proliferated through the early modern period, the question of arrangement or classification grew more and more pressing, and it was one that was also faced by the compilers of books. A book is a physical arrangement somewhere between a physical cabinet of specimens and a theoretical structure, or taxonomy. Decisions must be made concerning the placement and ordering of specimens, and moreover there are fewer opportunities for three-dimensional arrangement.

Gessner's encyclopedic ambition for the whole animal kingdom, it would seem, came to be seen as an overly ambitious task, at least when it came to producing fresh pictures. The whole animal kingdom was rarely again attempted within a single volume. Instead, natural groupings were pursued. Salviani limited himself to aquatic creatures in the mid-sixteenth century, a grouping which – perhaps needless to point out – is not the same as 'fishes'. Topsell's second volume, *The History of Serpents* (first published 1608), with its promisingly specific title, includes alongside asps and the like crocodiles, dragons, wasps, bees, and frogs. The underlying order for such a grouping was primarily theological.[29] William Turner produced the first-ever book devoted solely to birds in 1544. Turner, a friend of Gessner, planned to have his volume illustrated but in the event did not manage to do so.[30] After some time, birds would come to dominate the illustrated taxa.

The predominance of fish in early natural histories may perhaps speak to the excitingly alien nature of the underwater realm. There is also a satisfaction in preserving, through art, a creature which quickly dies, and noisomely decomposes, in the terrestrial realm. Sea creatures could rarely be kept in saline tanks in the way

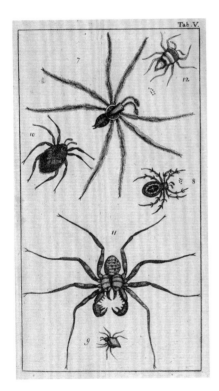

Spiders. Martin Lister,
Tractatus dei araneis (this plate from German edition, *Naturgeschichte der Spinnen*, Blankenburg, 1778)

Lister's first volume on spiders was a fairly conventional natural history, covering morphology, behaviour, biology, and lore. The second volume was taxonomic, employing both anatomical distinctions (number of eyes), and behavioural (methods of obtaining prey).

that elephants or giraffes could be kept in menageries; only in pictures could they be inspected at leisure. It is a great achievement to complete the task of visual record in time. The widowed Sarah Bowdich (1791–1856) was a master of the art; she made her artistic living by catching and painting over 3,000 fish, all on the river bank. In the early modern period, fish, and the marine realm more broadly, had direct economic value. In an era of voyages for trade, discovery, slavery, and plunder the sea creature indirectly emblematised great economic ventures. The strange fish is a token of puissant success and profit.

Fish aside, the choice of animal types for illustration was most powerfully intertwined with the types that were chosen for collection. Shells – graced with their own 'ology' in 1776 – were one easily stored and displayed item, scarcely subject to the processes of decay. They received extensive visual treatment, with increasing accuracy. One aspect of this accuracy – or, to begin with, inaccuracy – had to do with the medium of reproduction. Shells have a shared, natural chirality – a preferred direction of curling – but by default the process of engraving naturally reverses the original as recorded in first drawing. In the mid-eighteenth century standards of accuracy, developed in tandem with more exacting identification, were enhanced, and at this point the plates began to be routinely corrected for lifelikeness in the printed version.[31]

Insects, in the capacious early-modern sense of the word that included spiders and more, were even more important in the practices of collection and identification. They were relatively easy to preserve, and in many cases – most particularly butterflies – were of considerable aesthetic value. Gessner had in fact planned a book on insects, but it was via a very circuitous route that this was eventually published as Thomas Moffett's *Insectorum sive minimorum animalium theatrum* ('Insects, or the Theatre of Lesser Creatures') in 1634. Susanna and Anne Lister produced many engravings for their father's books on spiders and shells during the early years of the Royal Society, making their father the 'first arachnologist'.[32] During the 1710s, Eleazar Albin succeeded in drumming up support for a collection of 100 copper plates of English insects, each inscribed with a dedication to its individual subscriber – and so on. The undisputed monarch of the insect artists, however, must be Maria Sybilla Merian.

Like the *Historia piscium*, this book
was completed by Willughby's friend
Ray. And like Lister's work on spiders, it
attempts to prioritise questions of
taxonomy, dividing the birds, primarily,
into those of land and water. Land birds
are then divided into those with crooked
beaks and those with straight beaks;
water birds are divided into waders,
swimmers, and intermediate kinds.

John Ray (1627–1705) was probably the first person to foreground the question of taxonomy (as opposed to choosing an order *en passant*) in his books of natural history. Much of Ray's work, as for so many other natural historians, was concerned with plants. However, in 1672 Ray took on the work left uncompleted by his friend, Francis Willughby, at his death. This work was a *historia* of the birds, and another of fish. Although Ray drew extensively on many of the Renaissance writers noted above, he intended to create something quite new and different.[33] This was not to be a collection of all knowledge, both true and fabulous, nor yet an epitome of the creature. Instead it was to be a perfected, *natural* history, that reflected the beautiful order present in God's mind when he created the various kinds of animal. For Ray, the problem had arisen in Babel; human language had become corrupted in the Fall and its consequences. Adam's perfect, prelapsarian naming of the animals had become muddied by a profusion of languages and confused descriptions: by duplication and ambiguity. Once again, we hear the echoes of that pleasurable alphabetical game.

Florence the fish lives in Florida.

Engraving of Linnaeus.
William MacGillivray,
A History of British Quadrupeds,
Vol. 13 in Jardine's The Naturalist's
Library, London, 1843

Victorian readers collected images not
only of animals and birds, but also of
natural historians. Carolus Linnaeus was
recommended to the self-improving
readers of the *Penny Cyclopedia* (1839)
as a hard worker whose interest in
natural history 'neither poverty
nor misery was ... able to shake'.
The resultant moral directive did
not need spelling out.

God's perfect language, the book of nature, was written on the beasts themselves, and it was the task of the natural historian to read those signs aright, and re-inscribe them into scientific language. Thus Ray judged fins to be the proper sign of the fish. Hippopotami, traditionally drawn among aquatic creatures, were definitively excluded (likewise otters and frogs, which had previously been acceptable Lenten fare, being aquatically distinguished from animal flesh). On the downside, whales were now included, a fact which caused Ray some unease. Sub-divisions within the fish, and then other sub-divisions within those, further defined the natural order – that is, reflected the divine order. The whales were safely grouped with other cetaceans, leaving cartilaginous and bony fish as the two other main groups.

Just as the Lincei had begun to seek internal morphology among the plants some fifty years earlier, so now animal classification was placed on an anatomical footing. The many and careful engravings that illustrated Ray's book conveyed natural signs in non-linguistic form. Ray was not sure about the overarching value of pictures, but in the event was pleased with them, noting their 'conformity with the archetype of a fish or with a fish itself'.[34] At least eighteen engravers had been involved, reworking pre-existing images (notably Salviani's). Unfortunately, the feat almost broke the Royal Society, which had bankrolled publication. The pictures disastrously increased the cost of production, and the 500 or so copies failed to sell.

During the eighteenth and nineteenth centuries, other attempts to find a natural classification system were pursued. That of Carolus Linnaeus (1707–1778) is now the most celebrated, of course, but it was by no means universally or immediately accepted. Thomas Pennant (1726–1798), for example – a star writer of late eighteenth-century natural history – refused it. The quinarian system was a popular alternative in Britain during the early Victorian period. This divided animal kinds each into five groups, with analogies pertaining between equivalent groups in different taxa. The system was popular, among other reasons, because it yielded exciting predictions about species that might be discovered to fill missing groups. Books of animals reflected these various theories of classification, often promising in their subtitles that they were 'systematically arranged'. One might note that even Darwinism, the more-or-less correct answer to the question of taxonomy, does not provide any definitive pattern for the arrangement of creatures within the pages of a book.

As athletes get faster, so finish-line technology has to be made more accurate. Similarly, as the volume of scientific activity increased in the nineteenth century, so the judgements of priority hung on ever thinner margins. Unfortunately for natural historians, the practices of image publication did not always make attribution easy. During the nineteenth century – a period of intense natural-historical activity – collections of animal pictures were often issued in parts (monthly or quarterly). The images were generally dated by the figures on the wrappers of the parts, not the component pictures, or even by the bindings on the books that were ultimately made from the parts. This made priority in naming extremely difficult to adjudicate.[35]

Some kinds of animal, and some geographies, lend themselves more easily to completeness than others. There are not many kinds of mammal in Britain, for example, but uncountable varieties of beetle in the New World. (In fact, even counting British Coleoptera would be a considerable challenge.) As the scientific novelty of various natural kinds was exhausted, fresh questions were posed, either concerning new habitats, or more obscure taxa, or else in the realms of physiology, evolution, ecology, and ethology. Collections of well-established animal types, and unusual spottings (of rare or visiting species), passed into the realm of hobby, and hence popular publication.

In some cases, the professionalisation of natural history made the picture less desirable, less cutting-edge. The nineteenth century was not visually driven in many

Cover, Carl Vogt and F. Shecht,
Mammalia, Part 18 of
*The Natural History of Animals in
Word & Picture*, London, 1887–8

Visually speaking, the composite
portraiture of the Mammalia on the
cover of this partwork, together with
the decorative details, recalls the
conventions of the photographic
family album. This complemented
the domestic approach to the
Mammalia as characterised by their
family life. Animals chosen for full-page
illustrations were tried-and-tested
exotic species.

fields; the standard for patenting, for example, was not that an invention could be rendered as a diagram, but that it should be describable in words. Thus the need for pictures in natural history – at least for the purposes of identification – became, for some, the mark of the amateur; at the turn of the twentieth century, one lepidopterist remarked that he was glad to have been educated by Stainton's unadorned manual on the topic and not by the 'spoon food' of coloured plates.[36] Others embraced the challenge of zoological visualisation for the amateur as well as for the expert. The first keyed handbook – a book of beetles – was published in 1874. Its innovation was to lead its users through the visual grammar of the Coleoptera, step by step, choice by choice, until they had reached the correct identification.[37] The twentieth century saw the development of the Observer series (founded 1937) and other pocket guides, which sometimes grouped animals or birds by location, size, and shape for the convenience of the amateur.

The role of pictures in identification, and in the development of taxonomy, has been important, but it has not been their only one. If the story of animal pictures is told as part of the story of animal classification, the importance of artists recedes into the background. They become, simply, *illustrators* of theories dreamt up by thinkers and writers. Their names are forgotten as the authors' are remembered; they do not even appear on library catalogues. In the power of authors and publishers to arrange pictures, there was power to shape knowledge of the natural world as well as the story of its discovery. Artists who presumed to publish under their own name are demoted to the rank of 'mere' artists, at a tangent to the actual story of science. Important though the story of classification is, it is just a part of the larger history of animals in pictured form. The histories of collection, aesthetics, and economic value of the pictures themselves, and the books that act as their vehicles, are at least as important.

Dying to draw

In Helen Macdonald's bestselling 2014 memoir, 'H' is, as her title runs, 'for hawk'. It is a childlike designation that has mostly gone unremarked: a cosy title that belies the book's emotionally demanding contents. *H is for Hawk* is, in fact, a book about the author's grief and depression following the death of her father, and her recovery through her adoption and training of a goshawk. H is also for Helen. Despite its superficial unlikeliness, there is a certain psychological logic to the book's title, for the collection of animals is on one level a response to death. By killing something one pre-empts and thus manages the grief of death coming unannounced and accidentally – whether that feared death should befall the animal itself, or – by substitution – some other beloved object. How else to make sense of the passionate love that underpins the wildlife-watching of Victorian hunters, climaxing in the death of the animal?

As a young man, the controversial ornithologist Richard Meinertzhagen (1878–1967) was attached to the 3rd (East African) Battalion of the King's African Rifles, in which capacity he was posted to Kenya in the very earliest years of the twentieth century. His diaries are clotted with death, both animal and human. On one level, there is visible sentiment. Many of his entries report genuine distress at the brutality of colonisation, including the revenge killings he himself was 'compelled' to carry out – of entire villages, women and all. Moreover, he reports a great fondness for his pet tortoiseshell cat and dog, Baby, both with him in the field, and risks his life to save a monkey that is being tortured by some sailors.[38] Yet at other times Meinertzhagen succeeds in drawing down the blinds of objectivity, for example writing on 20 May 1902:

> I was out again today and soon came across a herd of Thomson's gazelle … After running about a quarter of a mile I managed to get close to [one] … and killed him. I came across a large number of human skeletons this afternoon … I brought home two or three good specimens.[39]

Here, Meinertzhagen succeeds in transferring his sanguine attitude towards game onto human beings, treating remains of the latter, just like lion skins or elephant tusks, as scientific trophies.

It often seems as though, in killing animals, Meinertzhagen is inoculating himself against the sentimental distress that would otherwise have overwhelmed when human and animal death was forced upon him. Historians of nineteenth-century science have identified the birth of the ideal of 'objectivity' in this period, portraying it in ways that resonate with Meinertzhagen's experience.[40] They describe how the production of a 'view-from-nowhere' or 'God's eye view' entailed a dramatic disciplining of the emotional, subjective self. In order to present a trustworthy account of nature 'as it really is', scientists and authors had to persuade their peers and readers that their own human sentiment and partiality had been well and truly crushed – put out of the picture. Nowhere is this more obviously true than in the field of natural history. In this science, objectivity entailed the killing of the self, specifically, the self that would otherwise be entangled – sentimentally, ecologically – with the killed animal specimen. Killing the animal was therefore a way of killing part of the self, of conspicuously demonstrating objectivity.

The killing of the creature does not mitigate the love that the observer feels for it. It is, according to some, even an expression of that love. 'He' – not it – 'is a beautiful creature,' wrote Meinertzhagen of a red lynx, 'with nice tufts of hair on his ears.'[41] He was contemplating its corpse after shooting it dead. Such expressions of 'love' are heard even in the present. The ecologist Craig Packer reported (in the *Observer* newspaper in 2015) visiting a 'tableau of death' in the mansion of billionaire lion-hunter Steven Chancellor. As Packer contemplated the more than fifty stuffed lions in the collection, Chancellor told him, 'As you can see, I have a special love of lions.'[42]

Shooters, collectors, naturalists – call them what you will – very often took what seems, from today's perspective, a sick pride in killing the last specimens of a rare species. The last Chatham fernbird, for example, was shot for the collection of Lionel Walter Rothschild in the Chatham Islands archipelago in 1895. Why record this, if not as a matter of pride? The species had been discovered less than thirty years previously; by 1900, with no further examples having been seen, it was declared extinct. Of course, with a small bird, it

Chatham Island black robin, Stephens Island wren, Chatham fernbird. Lionel Walter Rothschild, *Extinct Birds*, London, 1907

Rothschild accidentally self-commemorates in this image from his book *Extinct Birds*. Although he ascribes the extinction of the Chatham fernbird to rats, cats, and weasels – and is in general correct about this – other authorities consider that the last known survivor of the species was actually shot by Rothschild's collectors.

Great auk.
Lionel Walter Rothschild,
Extinct Birds, London, 1907

The great auk, along with the passenger pigeon, was among the many species shot in the nineteenth and twentieth centuries whose passing was commemorated – or perhaps celebrated – in this succinctly titled book.

was impossible for Rothschild to tell whether 'his' bullet actually took out the final living example. With larger trophies, there was a good chance of knowing what one was about even as one raised one's gun barrel. The wealthy Charles William George St John (1809–1856) gunned his way round Scotland, shooting what must have been very nearly the last breeding female osprey in the wild: 'I might have a chance of shooting the old osprey herself,' he recalled shortly after the event. 'I must say that I would rather she had escaped this fate; but as her skin was wanted, I agreed to try to kill her.'[43]

The last great auk was killed, in full knowledge of the act, on 3 June 1844. The species had been hunted in its millions around the northern hemisphere for food and feathers, and as its numbers declined, collectors began to seek auk corpses and eggs all the more ferociously for their scarcity value. One final colony of around fifty birds was discovered in 1835, on a remote Icelandic island. Their very rarity hung a fatal target mark upon them; museums quickly began collecting – that is, killing – birds from the colony.[44] The very last pair was strangled by three fishermen, hunting on behalf of a merchant. They smashed the pair's egg with their boots.

Upsetting though such stories are, it is difficult to hold them in mind when we contemplate a collected specimen in a museum. Martha the passenger pigeon is a case in point. The last authenticated wild-living member of her species was shot in 1900; Martha, a domestic specimen, was given to Cincinnati Zoo in 1902 and lived on until 1914. Upon her death her body was preserved and displayed at the Smithsonian Institution. Today, her body is a token of attempted preservation – in taxidermy if not in life – that exempts its viewers and its makers from moral culpability. That culpability is reserved for those invisible villains responsible for birds that no longer exist. Martha's body has become an icon that speaks for a narrative exactly opposite to her autobiography: it takes its place in a story of preservation and conservation, rather than of death.

As for real bodies, so it is for pictures. A pictured animal is generally a dead animal, an animal that has been killed and collected. Even if some animals were painted from a living specimen, the eighteenth- or nineteenth-century expedition as a whole was very often entangled in death. Mark Catesby's birds were mostly painted from life, but they fed a culture of trade and collection whose participants also purchased dead specimens. Moreover, collectors of the eighteenth century imported animals for their private menageries. Some survived, some did not; they almost never bred and so in this Darwinian sense of procreation were killed off. The trail of death extended to humans too. As exotic new species were collected and portrayed, human slaves were killed also, transported to and from the same places, profiting in many cases the very same people who subscribed to zoological portfolios. Catesby knew full well that the North American fauna was being transformed by the importation of new slave-raised crops. His interests in acclimatisation and the transplantation of species and varieties were keenly attuned to the mixing of human races, and of animal and plant varieties and species, that had occurred as a result of the trade between Africa and the New World colonies. The occasion for his studies was death-dipped economics.

Encounters with animal life became bloodier and bloodier as the nineteenth century unfolded. 'Collecting the set' had its darker side, most particularly in colonial history. Hunting, long a necessary means of subsistence for the many and sport for the few, became fatally linked to the projects of science and empire in the nineteenth century. Its primary practitioners were soldiers. In many ways they were the perfect collectors: they had the physical strength necessary for fieldwork and the field skills of tracking; they had the authority to command both European and African persons to act as their support staff. They had the military discipline to catalogue, precisely, where specimens had been shot – to the extent that their data is used by ecologists today to track the movement of species' populations. And finally, they had networks through which they could prepare and return specimens back to their own countries of origin.

The conquests of Asia and Africa provided the *mise en scène* for the elaboration of a code of masculinity conspicuously demonstrated by the shooting of animals.[45] Besides displaying a particular construction of gender, the hunting cult also represented an assumption of previously aristocratic rights by the middle classes. Where once the killing of deer was restricted to persons of noble birth, now distant continents provided the opportunity for middle-class men to do the same; if they could not rule at home, they could rule abroad. Besides providing a code and a rationale for colonialism, hunting also directly subsidised it and made it profitable, through the trade in animal trophies.

In this context, books of animal images again changed their function, adding to their previous roles the possibility of acting as a field guide. By the mid-nineteenth century, books were steam-printed and generally a cheaper commodity than their lovingly produced predecessors. One result of this was that they could be taken into the savannah, highlands, or wherever else the naturalist might go, being both physically smaller and less in need of protection from mud, rain, and so forth. Meinertzhagen complained in 1902 that he was 'badly handicapped by having no book on the birds of East Africa' with him in Kenya, so that he had no idea of what he was seeing, nor 'which [were] interesting and which [were] common'.[46] This suggests that having such a book to hand was the norm. One strongly suspects that Meinertzhagen coped with the problem by shooting everything and finding out later.

A natural history of the nests and eggs of British birds, printed in three volumes between 1853 and 1856, is one example of a user's guide. Its author, the clergyman-naturalist F. O. Morris, was passionately opposed to the destruction of nature in any form; indeed, as his biographer notes, 'his letters to The Times on bird protectionism became so numerous that he republished them as a small book'.[47] And yet it is highly likely that Morris' books were used to identify eggs pilfered from nests in the wild. The book itself was rather large and precious to take into the field – but eggs were easily brought home to compare against its pictures. Perhaps it even inspired its readers to seek out new and rarer eggs to steal. One can imagine fathers and sons bonding together over the act of collection, the sons providing the legwork and barked shins, the fathers providing the expensive book that gilded boyish hobbies with the patina of educational value. Most ironically of all for Morris, the pictures that were made for his *History of British Birds* were used by taxidermists as models to create lifelike stuffs. It was an example of the unintended effects of the nineteenth-century craze for natural history; where naturalists went, men with guns followed – often occupying the very same pair of boots. 'Ornithology,' writes David Allen of the late nineteenth

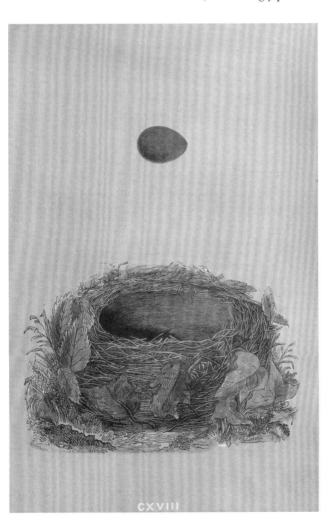

Nightingale's nest and egg. F. O. Morris, *A Natural History of the Nests and Eggs of British Birds*, London, 1853–6

This innocent-looking image, egg floating miraculously above nest like a saint in a Renaissance painting, actually speaks to the destructive hobby of egg collection in the nineteenth century.

Redhead duck.
Alexander Pope,
*Upland Game Birds and Water Fowl
of the United States*,
New York, 1878

Besides this much-reproduced
volume of pictures, Pope produced
a ten-part collection of *Celebrated
Dogs of America*, and successfully
made the transition to a portrait
painter of humans.

century, 'had substantially taken on the appearance of an adjunct to the gun-room of the typical country mansion.'[48]

In the late-nineteenth-century United States, sporting – that is, hunting – images were particularly successful. Alexander Pope's *Upland Game Birds and Water Fowl of the United States* (1878) and A. B. Frost's *Shooting Pictures* portfolio (1895) are especially fine examples. The hunting-based activity of nineteenth-century natural history was reproduced using a new medium: chromolithography. Reprints of Old Masters were common at the higher end of its quality spectrum. Made using oil-based inks, they hung proudly on the walls of middle-class homes. Expensive images drawn from nature (not art) were most often created using translucent, water-based inks, mimicking the original watercolours of naturalists. They were sold separately, in portfolios, such as the multi-artist *Sport, or Fishing and Shooting*, whose contents were intended to be framed. As such the images were often sold pre-trimmed, with the artist's name and picture title removed.

The North American landscape was being redesigned for tourists mimicking the activities glorified in such pictures, with the creation of national parks. The earliest users of these reserves tended to enjoy both kinds of shooting (cameras and guns) interchangeably – Theodore Roosevelt being perhaps the most famous, and promiscuous, shooter of the early twentieth century. Fashions, however, slowly changed. US and European zoos grew in popularity, and were re-angled towards juvenile visitors. Family films and television programmes, based around such zoos as well as wild animals, blossomed. All this made game hunting an increasingly distasteful prospect for the average person. Instead, in Africa, conservation reserves were carved out of the game reserves created and policed for the invading colonial elites. By the 1930s, these wildlife preserves were being used for the purpose of allowing tourists to shoot animals with their cameras, creating photographic collections. Pictures such as appeared in the magazine *National Geographic* were far preferable for the average reader, unable to afford such trips for him or herself.

Even modes of collection that do not depend on direct killing have something of Meinertzhagen's emotional logic about them. Alphabetical filing, scientific taxonomy, or even drawing all remove the animal cognitively from the materiality of real encounter. These actions kill off the animal's agency, its noise, its smell: its insistently animal nature. The creature is transmogrified into specimen, into picture, into representative of a taxon. It lives on eternally as memory or as data. Hence the curious sense that the birth of one panda in a zoo is a great cause for celebration – more so than a well-established and secure breeding community in the wild would be. It seems to us that so long as there is one (or, we must concede biologically, a pair), the species is safe, enclosed in our collections. To create a specimen, something must have died. That this sequence of events should be a positive thing is the myth of Noah.

The direction of this logic reaches its end in the work of photographer Joel Sartore. In 2005, supported by the *National Geographic*, Sartore began a 25-year project to photograph every one of the 12,000 species held in captivity, half of which are predicted to disappear in the current mass extinction caused by humans. Entitled *The Photo Ark* – Noah again – Sartore's project has resulted in extraordinary and stunning pictures which eerily recapitulate the range of media available through history, from high-quality, high-price fine art prints, through to the democratised genres of the illustrated calendar or the mass-produced poster. Well-intentioned in its awareness-raising, and extraordinary in its artistic calibre, the project nevertheless unsettles in its substitution of virtual collection for real preservation.

I think of what wild animals are in our imaginations. And how they are disappearing – not just from the wild, but from people's everyday lives, replaced by images of themselves in print and on screen. The rarer they get, the fewer meanings animals can have. Eventually rarity is all they are made of. The condor is an icon of extinction … It is a shadow, a figure of loss and hope; it is hardly a bird at all.[49]

A paper zoo is very often beautiful; but it is also a catalogue of death.

Stuffed animals galore in Bullock's Museum, shown in R. Ackermann, *The Repository of Arts, Literature, Commerce, Manufactures, Fashions and Politics*, London, 1823–8

Animals, alive and dead, were a popular entertainment of the eighteenth and nineteenth centuries. Bullock was an entrepreneur who had moved his collection from Liverpool to the greater opportunities of London. He attracted visitors by means of the 'artificial forest' seen in this illustration, which contained an array of 'larger Quadrupeds, Birds and Reptiles'.

Drawing for all

The nineteenth century saw an explosion in the range, quality, and quantity of books published. The introduction of the steam-driven printing press was one major factor in this cultural shift; it made books far quicker and cheaper to print. Changing duties on paper, cheaper paper manufacture, and relaxed controls on publication all eased up the market. Literacy rose to meet these changes, and benevolent organisations subsidised the making and lending of books to the new, working-class reading public. Pictures of animals found a new home in these books; natural histories were a popular choice for an improving read.

The printer William Lizars (1788–1859) very quickly saw the market potential for a very low-priced series on natural history, based on the same model of cheap, uniform volumes that was used for Walter Scott's Waverley novels or multi-volume encyclopedias. The Naturalist's Library was, despite its title, entirely devoted to animals. Lizars saw a plenitude of colour illustrations as integral to its success; the prospectus promised that all would be specially commissioned and newly drawn.[50] Fourteen volumes duly appeared in the ten years from 1833. At 6 shillings per volume (around £15 in today's money) they were indeed affordable by the middle classes, and even by workers. Lizars managed thirty to forty engravings per volume, not including woodcuts. His success was partly due to the cheaper production costs in his native Edinburgh, but mostly to tremendous discipline and professionalism. The standard run on each volume was 1,000 copies, though some sold many more.

As the century progressed a leisured middle class, with disposable income, emerged. David Allen has brilliantly described the Victorians' succession of crazes in natural history, hobbies that were in no small part facilitated by the development of railway travel to rural and seaside places.[51] Amateur drawing and painting of natural historical subjects flourished. A wealth of books appeared, most especially in the 1850s and 60s, to support and profit from this fashion. What ferns were to botany – producing a so-called 'pteridomania' – so home aquaria were to seashore life. The Victorians rolled up their trousers, hitched up their skirts, and fished for molluscs and anemones, transporting them home and attempting to keep them alive in tanks filled with sea-water. Books such as Philip Gosse's *History of the British Sea-Anemones and Corals* informed and encouraged such activities, which unfortunately had noticeably damaging effects on biodiversity in some places. Microscopes became a widely owned gadget for enhancing natural-historical activity, and drawings that were either directly microscopic, or aesthetically or representationally related to microscopic diagramming, became part of the visual lexicon of ordinary readers.

Lizars' high-risk strategy of tempting readers with new pictures was not emulated by all. Many publishers re-used earlier plates in the making of their books. At high volumes of production, hand colouring was no longer practicable, and black and white images had to suffice unless the cost of chromolithography was warranted, usually just for a few special plates. Authorship, too, was sometimes hasty and of lower originality than might have been hoped. Despite the fact that pictures were often considered to be the feature that attracted readers, it was the names of authors that were associated with titles; they became their flags of convenience when it came to recognition

'Narwhal'.
Title page, Robert Hamilton, *Mammalia* Vol. 6, *The Natural History of the Ordinary Cetacea or Whales*, The Naturalist's Library, London, 1843

Hamilton begins his survey of whales with an account of their anatomy. As per the French savant Cuvier, he thinks of the fin as 'converted from an arm', without, however, meaning this in any evolutionary sense. Rather God was responsible for the gradations of design within each of the great animal classes.

and saleability. The public lecturer J. G. Wood, though little known today, reigned supreme among these names, though in his case not without artistic merit too; he was noted for his ability to draw brilliantly while speaking to an audience. Wood was snapped up by the publishers of Routledge's Railway Library, a series of cheap books sold at railway stations for reading on trains. Wood naively signed away his copyrights for small sums, unaware that his books would sell (or had sold) so well: over 10,000 copies in the very first week for *Common Objects of the Country* (1858). The cheapness and small size of books such as Wood's meant that they could be taken into the field for the purposes of identification. They were neither too cumbersome to carry, nor too precious to get a little wet or dirty.

The urge to collect items in the field was complemented by a new urge to collect sets of books about them. Publishers produced 'libraries' of zoology and botany to feed this craving and, as well as creating a sense of nature's scope, they created a history of natural history itself. Each volume would very often be prefaced with a biography and portrait of a historical expert in the field, adding a new dimension to what was collected.

By the very end of the nineteenth century, readers' tastes had changed. Experience-based narratives of nature became more popular than natural history in its own right. In the United States, John Burroughs (1837–1921) and Ernest Thompson Seton (1860–1946) fed an appetite for the return to nature, the romanticised Native American, and new models of childhood. In Britain, accounts of rambles in 'our country' and tales of an idyllic rural past sold well. Pictures, strangely, receded in importance, even despite the new possibilities offered by the camera. Perhaps photography out-reached itself; the new technology, though promising modernity, produced pictures that were frankly disappointing compared to what had gone before. It was quickly eclipsed by film, and then television, as the public's medium of choice for consuming nature.

The story of animal photography has echoed the slow conversion of Audubon's paintings from relatively niche products of science to valuable works of art. Only latterly, as photography has come to be appreciated as a valid form of visual art, have animal photographs come to have value in their own right. In 1965, when the BBC magazine *Animals* launched a photographic competition, it was firmly within the realm of nature fans. Adopted in 1984 by the Natural History Museum, its scientific nature was reasserted. Even now there is an element of curiosity, rather than artistic appreciation, in the responses provoked by winning entries. 'Fancy an animal doing that!' we remark, or perhaps, 'fancy being able to get that photo!' The ready accessibility of digital technologies, producing an ever larger pool of photographers, and the relatively lawless sharing of images on the Internet, have made the production of animal images as economically precarious as it ever was in the eighteenth century. Artists have responded with an eighteenth-century strategy: crowdfunding – the twenty-first-century equivalent of subscriptions. Thus, for example, Jack Perks, a young British photographer, raised £3,500 in 2015 to enable his project of photographing every freshwater fish species in Britain. It is a small sum compared with the great eighteenth- and nineteenth-century portfolios; the value of the medium has been economically degraded by the Internet, and the prestige value of the creatures portrayed has also changed and diminished. A picture of an exotic creature is no longer a token of privileged and profitable participation in the world of trade and commerce.

Aldrovandi's dream of creating Noachic completeness in a collection of physical animal specimens is long gone, but the urge to collect is as strong as ever. If a complete collection of nature is impossible, then artistic constraints (alphabetical, pictorial) can creatively frame an alternative meaningful set instead. Cassiano dal Pozzo's 'paper museum' passed through various hands, losing many of its components

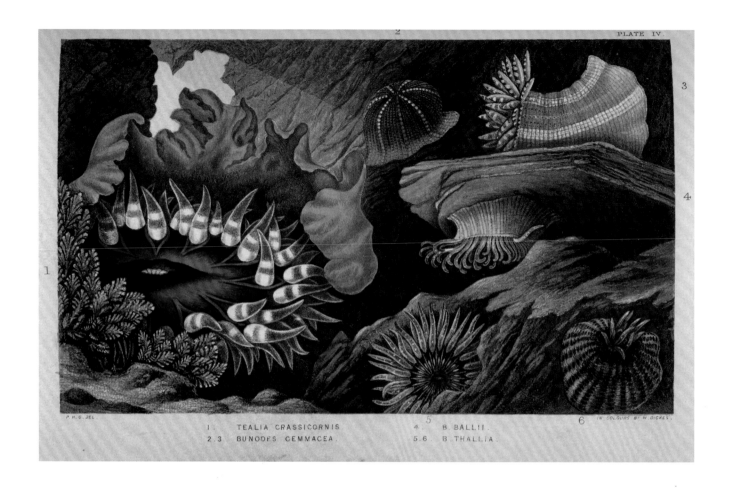

1. TEALIA CRASSICORNIS.   4.   B. BALLII.
2.3. BUNODES GEMMACEA.   5.6. B. THALIA.

along the way; it regained collectible value when it was purchased by George III (from a cardinal who needed a dowry for his mistress's daughter). Even after that, it continued to be mistreated and fragmented; its current re-consolidation and conservation by prestigious national bodies was initiated by the art historian and Soviet spy Anthony Blunt.[52] We all know the end of the Audubon story. After a phase of dispersal and dismissal, his books are now among the most valuable in existence, selling at auction for prices that rival those of even the rarest medieval codices. Even the humble Observer's guides are now collectible: a complete set is an extremely costly commodity. The recent Animal series, published by Reaktion Books since 2003 – each volume dedicated to a single animal kind – has inspired its own dedicated following of collectors. These final examples are, in fact, collections of collections – a circularisation of the process. The example you now hold in your hand is another in this historical series: it too is a paper zoo.

Zelda the zookeeper lives in Zimbabwe.

PLATE III.

OPPOSITE
Sea anemones.
*'Plate IV, Tealia crassicornis,
Bunooes cemmacea,
B. ballii, B. thallia'.*

RIGHT
Sea anemones.
*'Plate III, Sagartia troglogytes,
S. viduata, S. pallida, S. pura,
Adamsia palliata'.*
Both from Philip Henry Gosse,
Actinologia Britannica,
London, 1858–60

Gosse encouraged his readers to retrace the history of science and discover for themselves the remarkable truth that many plant-like organisms at the seashore are in fact animals. He described what they might expect to see under a microscope: 'in every cradle [cell] there lies a baby, with its little knees bent up to its chin … we see him gradually protruding his head … when lo! the head falls open, and becomes a bell of tentacles!'

P.H.G.DEL.

IN COLOURS BY W. DICKES.

1.2. SAGARTIA TROGLODYTES.   4.5. S. PALLIDA.

3. S. VIDUATA.   6. S. PURA.

7.8. ADAMSIA PALLIATA.

TESTUDO CARBONARIA. *Spix.*

½ long: nat:

J.D.C.Sowerby, del, E.Lear, lithog.

Printed by C.Hullmandel.

Exotic

Exotic animals were the quintessential animal type of the early modern period. From the very first European voyages of exploration, travellers began to stumble upon creatures that were not included in classical knowledge systems. There were new butterflies, fish, shells, mammals – all unknown to Pliny and Aristotle. New and exotic beasts – some colourful, some shy, some tragically approachable with a gun – were soon shipped back to Europe, where they formed the basis of vibrant economies. Whether alive in menageries, or stuffed and mounted in collections, they were very valuable commodities. Dried and stuffed, they were collected by princes and royalty, and displayed in great rooms where they spoke to the wealth and global reach of their collectors. Others were recorded in paintings, watercolours, and drawings.

The largest, fiercest, and most spectacular beasts were the most likely to be commemorated in paper form, as paintings, watercolours, or engravings. Dürer's famous engraving of the rhinoceros is perhaps the definitive animal image of the early modern period, yet still closely related to the paradoxical beasts and monsters celebrated by medieval bestiaries. It has the same extraordinary qualities; it is apparently quite unrelated to the familiar European animals of woodland and farmyard. Paintings of such creatures were traded as valuable specimens in their own right. Fish were a particularly suitable choice for visual record, collected in the course of foreign voyaging and hard to preserve in bodily form.

As the profits from the New World began to trickle down through society, creating a wealthy bourgeoisie of merchants, doctors, and lawyers, so the collectors of exotic beasts increased in number. An Amsterdam doctor could not easily collect stuffed sharks or giraffes, but insects were within his reach. Smaller displays – contained in ornate and highly decorated cabinets – were the new standard for exotic collection. Whereas princes had collected and traded unique paintings of rare beasts, now reproduced images – engravings and books – supported and complemented these bourgeois collections. Maria Sybilla Merian's gorgeous painted insects from Surinam were the perfect complement to a Dutch doctor's cabinet.

As the shapes of empire changed, so did the animal world and its visual inscription. The Anthropocene was well under way, with human-wrought ecosystemic changes afoot. Different world regions were encountered and exploited, and each in its turn provided a foreign fauna iconic to its era. During the eighteenth and nineteenth centuries, the East Indies, South Asia, the Caribbean, and the northern portion of the Americas all yielded fresh exotica for the British. This was the great era of coloured engravings; funded by subscription, these pictures signified their owners'

Red-footed tortoise
('*Testudo carbonaria*').
Lithograph by Edward Lear after a drawing by J. C. D. Sowerby, from Thomas Bell, *A Monograph of the Testudinata*, London, 1832–6

The author of this monograph on tortoises confessed that the reptiles 'cannot ... offer sources of amusement or interest' comparable to mammals. But Edward Lear's gorgeously realised lithographs bring some glamour to the *Testudinata*, with their geometric patterns and intricately coloured scales. One imagines that the young Lear found comedy as well as beauty in these shelly creatures.

participation in an international economy of natural history that was prestigious as well as profitable.

Meanwhile the creation of menageries – in private estates and for public touring – brought exotic creatures to wider and more various audiences. Zebras grazed the lawns of aristocrats, and peacocks picked their way through the flower beds. Ephemeral flyers drew ordinary people to metropolitan shows of rhinoceroses and elephants; and society painters commemorated their star creatures in oils. The cheap curiosity value of exotic beasts expanded with the birth of steam-printed images; prints of kangaroos and penguins distracted the working classes from their everyday experiences (and perhaps from political protest).

Of course, what is exotic to one person is perfectly familiar to another. It takes an outsider to class something as exotic, and to imbue it with cultural and economic rarity-value. Thus John J. Audubon's birds found their subscribers in Britain, not America. The unusual nature of the birds – and their bear-greased, outlandish recorder – pleased British collectors more than their American counterparts. Exotic creatures also, sometimes, came to blur in the European mind with the human inhabitants of far-flung lands. Narratives of travels in Africa unreflectively jumbled adventures with ants and 'natives' in a single fauna. Nineteenth- and twentieth-century museums and magazines mixed artefacts of anthropology and natural history without qualm.

Today, the world is small but the category of exotica remains firmly in place for European and North American audiences, an unexamined blend of provenance, colour, sound, and ferocity. Children's books create a single, ecologically nonsensical 'jungle' category in which savannah lions from Africa and jungle tigers from India all mix together with Amazonian birds and frogs.

PLATE. I.

R.Savery pinx   M&N Hanhart imp.   J Erxleben lith

DIDUS.

Bengal tiger.
Watercolour by a Calcutta artist, *c.* 1820.
Inscribed in pencil '*Felis Tigris – or Bengal tiger*'. Hastings Albums (collected by the Marquess of Hastings and Lady Hastings, Bengal, 1813–23)

The magnificent Bengal tiger has long been emblematic of the subcontinent, rivalling the (ecologically implausible) British lion. This rivalry has resulted in tensions – staged interspecies fights and imperial unease. Tenniel's cartoon for *Punch* during the Indian Rebellion (1857) showed 'The British lion's vengeance on the Bengal tiger'.

A. Specht lith.

H. Seeger imp.

THE LEOPARD. *(Felis Pardus.)*

Tigers ('*Felis tigris*').
Daniel Giraud Elliot,
A Monograph of the Felidae,
New York, 1878–83

The similarity between the great cats
and their harmless domestic cousins is a
source of pleasant reflection. The house
cat can be seen as a stealthy hunter,
or the tiger as a curled-up puss. Visual
representations such as this celebrate
that enjoyable tension.

FELIS TIGRIS.

'Elephant'.
Oliver Goldsmith,
*The History of the Earth
and Animated Nature,*
London, 1822

This statically portrayed elephant
embodies the quality of sagaciousness
that was most often attributed to the
animal. Stories and anecdotes abounded
to illustrate this supposed characteristic,
from finding food and protecting
family members to kneeling – in one
memorable instance – to greet the
Archbishop of Milan.

ELEPHANT.

Published by Henry Fisher, London 1822.

'*The Elephant*'.
Samuel Daniell,
*A Picturesque Illustration of the Scenery,
Animals, and Native Inhabitants of the
Island of Ceylon: In Twelve Plates
Engraved after Drawings, from Nature,
of Samuel Daniell*,
London, 1808

Samuel Daniell was unable to make his
living as a professional landscape painter
in Britain, and was obliged instead to take
postings to Africa and then Ceylon (now
Sri Lanka), in which latter place he was
appointed ranger of woods and forests.
No doubt he encountered many
elephants in this role.

THE ELEPHANT.

FOR A FEW DAYS ONLY!
LOCK'S FIELDS
Walworth, near the Salisbury Arms.

In consequence of

▌MR. HYLTON▐

Having made Extensive Alterations and Additions to the Menagerie, by Purchasing the most Handsome Quadruped in the World, namely,

THE ZEBRA, ALSO THE OURANG-OUTANG,
OR. MAN MONKEY.

The Noble Male Performing
ELEPHANT!
A Noble Male Caffrarian
LION,
And Untameable **HYENA,**
In One Den Together, in a state of Jealous Fondness
The Royal **Striped Bengal Tiger,**
The Hunting Leopardess,
And their TWO CROSS BRED CUBS, in One Den.
BLACK AND BROWN BEARS.
The Ravenous Wolf.

And many other
ANIMALS
Will induce him to remain some time longer in his present situation,
THE COATMUNDI; or ANT EATER:
Striped, Spotted and
LAUGHING HYENAS.
*Racoons from North America. The Pelicans
of the Wilderness, Male and Female,*
With a Variety of Others, of the Feathered Tribe.
Several Large Serpents.
Admission 1d.
J. W. PEEL, *Printer, 9, New Cut, Lambeth, opposite the Victoria.*

Playbill for Mr Hylton's Menagerie
at Lock's Fields, London, 1842

The East India Company was initially
responsible for introducing the British
public to live elephants. From the EIC's
ships the specimens would make their
way to menageries and other shows.
As historian Christopher Plumb records,
in 1675 a young male was exhibited at
Garraway's Coffee House for an entrance
fee of three shillings. This elephant would
reportedly use his trunk to 'punch either
man or beast that anger'd him'.

BELOW
Zebra.
Ebenezer Sibly,
*An Universal System of Natural History
Including the Natural History of Man, Etc.*,
London, 1794–1807

Like a horse in shape but dramatically
and differently coloured, the zebra was
a sure-fire exotic favourite as soon as
it was discovered. In this drawing the
stripe-signifiers have been imposed upon
the body without any need for observational
accuracy. The legs and neck have been
lengthened, too, to resemble the species
more familiar to Europeans.

Young Sumatran tapir.
Probably by J. Briois, March 1824.
Gouache on paper. From an album of
fifty-one drawings of birds and animals
made at Bencoolen, Sumatra for
Sir Stamford Raffles

Besides collecting this paper zoo,
Raffles helped to establish the
Zoological Society of London and its
Zoological Gardens (now London Zoo).

Werner del.

$\frac{1}{10}$

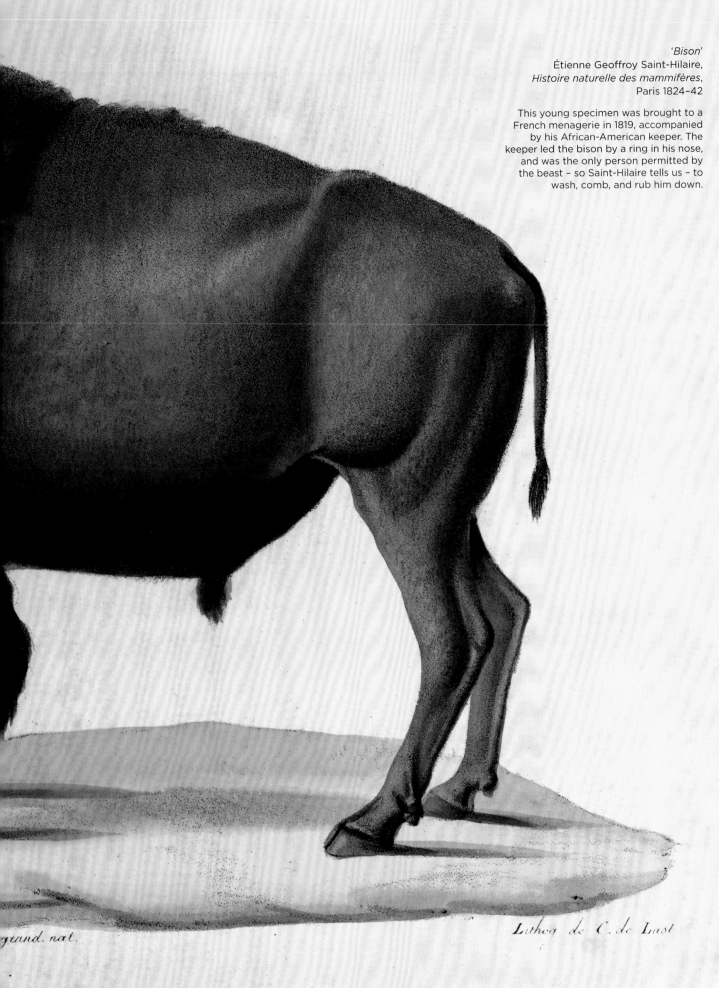

'*Bison*'
Étienne Geoffroy Saint-Hilaire,
Histoire naturelle des mammifères,
Paris 1824–42

This young specimen was brought to a
French menagerie in 1819, accompanied
by his African-American keeper. The
keeper led the bison by a ring in his nose,
and was the only person permitted by
the beast – so Saint-Hilaire tells us – to
wash, comb, and rub him down.

grand. nat.

Lithog de C. de Last

son

OPPOSITE
'The Giraffe'.
Royal School Series of Wall
Pictures, late nineteenth century

Until the mid-nineteenth century, the giraffe was commonly known as the cameleopard. This portmanteau word captured how the creature 'hathe the heed of a camell ... and speckes [spots] of the Perde [panther]', in the words of thirteenth-century encyclopedist Bartholomew de Glanville.

Javan rhinoceros, or lesser one-horned rhinoceros ('*Rhinoceros sondiacus*'). Watercolour by an anonymous Indian artist, collected in India in the 1820s by James Chicheley Hyde

Ever since Dürer produced his famous woodcut of the Indian rhinoceros brought to Portugal in 1515, the rhino – or its image – has functioned as the *fons et origo* of the exotic beast. This trotting specimen scarcely satisfies the viewer, so firmly fixed is Dürer's in the imagination.

THE GIRAFFE.

(No. V—"Royal School Series" of Wall Pictures.)

Gulb or harness antelope.
A plate by Edward Lear from
John Edward Gray, *Gleanings from the
Menagerie and Aviary at Knowsley Hall*,
privately printed, 1846

Edward Smith-Stanley, 13th Earl of Derby,
retired from politics to focus on building
up his collection at the magnificent
Knowsley Hall in Merseyside, England.
At his death in 1851 he had 345 living
mammals and 1,272 birds in his estate
grounds, including the Derbyan parakeet
named in his honour. Lear was employed
to capture many of them in pictorial form.

Gnu.
Samuel Daniell,
*A Collection of Plates Illustrative
of African Scenery and Animals*,
London, 1804–5

Used as we are to considering the lion
'king of the beasts', John Barrow's
representation of the 'gnoo' in this regal
position comes as a surprise. Yet during
his tour of the Cape of Good Hope –
where he was sent to calm political
relations – this was Barrow's conclusion.
'This extraordinary animal is the swiftest
beast that ranges the plains of Africa
... The gnoo might be considered as an
emblem of unbounded freedom with
the means of supporting it.'

Opossum and young, and life cycle
of the praying mantis.
Maria Sybilla Merian,
*Merian dissertatio de generatione et
metamorphosibus insectorum Surinamensium*
(includes French translation), The Hague, 1726

Maria Sybilla Merian is best known for her extraordinary
insect drawings and her work on insect metamorphosis
at the turn of the eighteenth century. She described the
behaviour of the Merian opossum, as it became known:
'When these rats come out of their hole, either to play
or to seek their food, they run about with their mother;
but when they are satisfied ... or are apprehensive
of danger, they climb up again on the back of their
mother, and twist their tails round that of the parent.'
Travelling alone with her daughter in South America,
perhaps she found the image a comforting or even a
proud emblem of self-sufficiency.

Zerda (fennec fox).
Ebenezer Sibly,
*An Universal System of Natural History
Including the Natural History of Man, Etc.*,
London, 1794–1807

The zerda may be commended to all clever
children as a triumphant conclusion to a round of
animal alphabets. Such children will wish to add
the following exotic facts: also known as fennec
foxes, zerdas are mountainous desert-dwellers
of Africa and the Middle East, and are smaller
than the average house cat.

Ethiopian wolf ('"*Kabaru*", *Canis simensis*').
Drawn by Louis Agassiz Fuertes from life,
Mt Albasso, 11 November 1926.
Louis Agassiz Fuertes and Wilfred Hudson Osgood,
Artist and Naturalist in Ethiopia [diaries kept on the
Field Museum–Chicago *Daily News* Ethiopian
Expedition], New York, 1936

Louis Agassiz Fuertes was best known for his
ornithological paintings, but this intimate portrait
indicates his abilities across species boundaries.
Fuertes was part of the first generation of natural
historians to occupy academic positions in the
United States; the trip on which this painting
was made was co-funded by the Chicago Field
Museum and the *Daily News*.

Orang-utan.
E. Donovan,
*The Naturalist's Repository,
or Monthly Miscellany of
Exotic Natural History*,
London, 1823–8

Charles Darwin famously encountered
an orang-utan at the London
Zoological Society shortly after this
picture was published. Her name was
Jenny and she was drinking from a
saucer. 'Let man visit Ouranoutang
in domestication, hear its expressive
whine, see its intelligence when
spoken to; as if it understands every
word said,' he mused, 'and then let
him boast of his proud pre-eminence.'
Queen Victoria limited her reaction
to noting that she found the species
'disagreeably human'.

Japanese macaque
('*Innuus speciosus*').
Philipp Franz von Siebold,
*Fauna Japonica sive descriptio
animalium quae in itinere
per Japoniam*,
Leiden, 1833–50

Fauna Japonica was the first book
written in a European language
(French) on the Japanese fauna.
It was based on the collections made
by Philipp Franz von Siebold, resident
physician and scientist to Dejima for
the Dutch East India Company, and his
successor, Heinrich Burger, in Japan.

OPPOSITE
Gelada baboons.
Louis Agassiz Fuertes and Wilfred
Hudson Osgood,
*Artist and Naturalist
in Ethiopia* [diaries kept on the
Field Museum–Chicago *Daily News*
Ethiopian Expedition],
New York, 1936

A result of the same expedition as the
Ethiopian wolf portrait (previous page),
this dramatic baboon landscape connects
visually with the theatrical dioramas then
being developed as modes of animal
display at the Chicago Field Museum and
American Museum of Natural History.

Mysore Coll. of Drawings

Black Monkey
Cephalopteus

Langurs ('*Black Monkey*' and '*White Monkey*'). Painted by an anonymous Indian artist in about 1802, for a volume created under the direction of the Rajah of Tanjore and presented to the court by Mr Benjamin Torin in 1807

John Lockwood Kipling (father of Rudyard) noted the mixed representations of monkeys in colonial India. 'Some of the respect in which these animals are held by Hindus is a reflection of the popularity of Hanuman ... the monkey general of the great Hindu epic ... A notion [also] exists among Hindus that the English may be his descendants through a female servant of the demon king ... Others, again, say that the English came from the "monkey army," which unlovely phrase is occasionally used to describe the British nation.'

White monkey

Ring-tailed lemur.
George Edwards,
*A Natural History of Uncommon Birds, and of
Some Other Rare and Undescribed Animals,*
London, 1743–51

This picture summons up the myth of the Fall:
the contemplated fruit, the lurking partner, the
curling, striped, snake-like tail. There is even a
banished creature disappearing off stage-left.
Edwards kept a 'Maucauco' (as the lemur was also
known) alive for a while in his home, finding it a
'very innocent, harmless Creature, having nothing
of the Cunning or Malice of the Monkey-Kind'.

OPPOSITE
Flying female lemur with young,
hanging from a branch.
Watercolour attributed to
a Chinese artist, *c.* 1800

This is one of the drawings collected by
William Marsden between 1784 and 1808
for a third edition of his *Natural History
of Sumatra*. Like many natural historians,
Marsden also collected cultural artefacts – in
his case, coins.

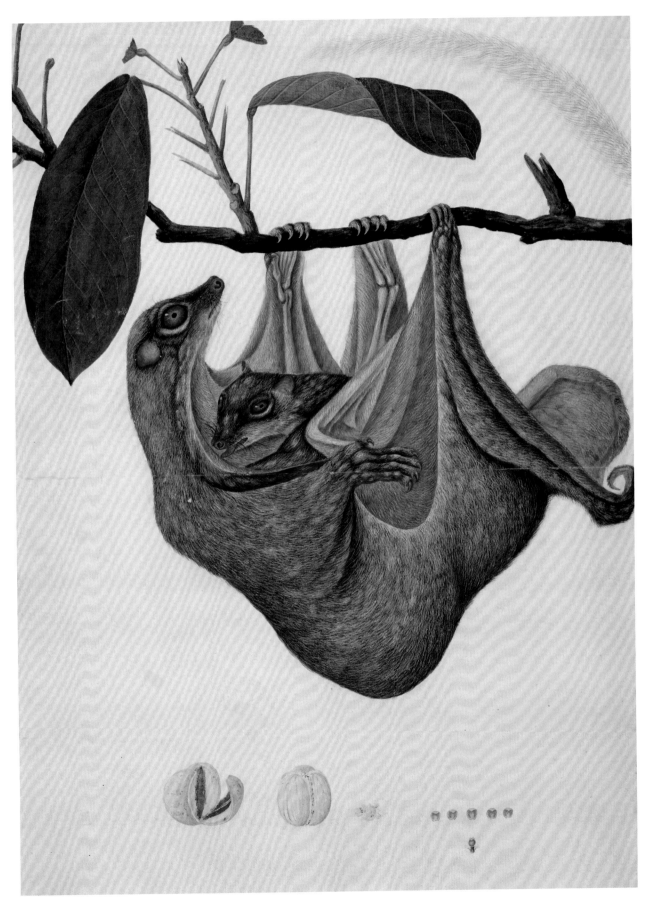

Giant armadillo ('*Priodontes gigas*').
Animaux nouveaux ou rares recueillis pendant
L'Expedition dans les parties centrales
de l'Amerique du Sud, Vol. 7 (*Zoologies.*
Mammifères) in Count du Castelnau,
Expedition dans les parties centrales de
l'Amerique du Sud, 1843

Along with anteaters and tree-sloths, armadillos are
today considered part of the superorder Xenarthra,
an unusual and primitive set of mammals found
only in South America.

Expédition de F. de Castelnau.(Amérique du Sud.)

7ᵉ Partie. Zoologie. Mammifères. Pl.18.

Werner.Lith.

P. Bertrand, éditeur.

Lith. Gény-Gros. Paris.

PRIODONTES GIGAS

Sloth.
Albert Seba,
*Locupletissimi rerum naturalium
thesauri accurata descriptio*,
Amsterdam, 1734–65

Seba's collection was one of the
bases upon which Linnaeus started to
develop his classification system.

'*Lesser Ant-bear or Eater*'.
Artist and date unknown;
from a volume of natural history
drawings in the collection of
Sir Joseph Banks

Joseph Banks was, in his early
life, an adventurer, ladies' man,
and collector, sailing with Captain
Cook in his first voyage on the HMS
Endeavour (1768–71). In later life
Banks was a patron, collector, and
éminence grise of science.

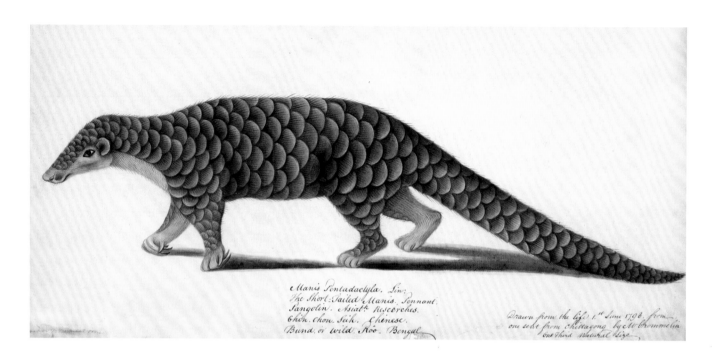

Manis Pentadactyla. Lin:
The Short-Tailed Manis. Pennant.
Sangolin. Asiat. Researches.
Chin. chou. Siih. Chinese.
Bund. or wild. Koo. Bengal.

Drawn from the life 1.st June 1798. from
one sent from Chittagong by M. Brommetin
one third Natural Size.

Pangolin. Inscribed '*Manis Pentadactyla. Lin. The Short Tailed Manis – Pennant. Pangolin Asiatic Reserches. Chin Chow Seik Chinese. Bund or Wild Roo – Bengal. Drawn from life 1st June 1796 from one sent from Chittagong by M Crommelin. One Third Natural Size.*' Marquess Wellesley Collection of Natural History Drawings

Shortly after this drawing was made, a coat and helmet covered in pangolin scales and leafed in gold were presented to King George III by the East India Company's Governor-General of Bengal. The pangolin's natural protection – alas no use against the EIC – was whimsically rendered as human armour.

Great anteater.
George Shaw,
Musei Leveriani explicatio, Anglica et Latina (containing select specimens from the museum of the late Sir Ashton Lever, Kt., with descriptions in Latin and English),
London, 1792

The naturalist John Ray counted the exotic ant-bear (anteater) as evidence for God's providential creation: 'Being kept tame, they are fed with Flesh, but it must be minced small, because they have not only a slender and sharp Head and Snout, but also a narrow and toothless Mouth; their Tongue is like a great Lute-string (as big as a Goose-quill) round ... and therefore lies doubled in a Channel between the lower Parts of the Cheeks. This when hungry they thrust forth, being well moistened, ... and when it is covered with Ants, suddenly draw it back into their Mouths; if the Ants lie so deep that they cannot come at them, they dig up the Earth with their long and strong Claws, wherewith for that Purpose their Fore-feet are armed. So we see how their Parts are fitted for this Kind of Diet, and no other.'

Alligator.
Artist and date unknown; from a volume of natural history drawings in the collection of Sir Joseph Banks

Alligators are native to America and China. They are to be distinguished from crocodiles by their teeth – by artists brave enough to approach closely.

Gharial ('*Lacerta Gangetica or Gangetic Crocodile*').
Watercolour by Sita Ram, *c.* 1820

The first Western description of this species, in 1759, mistook an accidental hole on the abdomen for a ventral pouch such as is possessed by the opossum (page 60) for holding its young. Here it is face to face with a grasshopper.

the difference tile he told me of it after dinner.

The Kangaroos when taken young, become in very short time quite domestic and
familiar, there are now in many families some very fine large ones, they live on
bread, corn and grass, they use their fore paws in eating but when they move they
use only the hind legs, and they run amazing fast, when resting the sit erect and
bear on the last joints of the hinder legs, the under parts of which are firm and cal=
lous like a hoof, their tail which is strong & muscular they use as a weapon of
defence, and when pursued very close they annoy and hurt the dogs very much
with it.

is the most curious and singular animal I have ever seen, the one from which I
have taken the drawing is one foot, eleven inches & half from the point of the bill to
the end of the tail, eleven inches in the round of the thickest part of the body and four
inches & half in the length of the tail from the anus, it is web footed, on the fore foot
is five nails or claws and one behind like the gaff of a cock not placed immediately
on its extremity, on its hind foot is five claws remarkably sharp and long and

Kangaroos and platypus.
From a journal kept on board
the *Minerva* transport ship
from Ireland to New South
Wales, 1798–1800; top of
page titled '*Ship Minerva,
Sidney Cove, Port Jackson,
New South Wales*'

The 'discovery' of Australia
occurred only one or two
generations into a serious
attempt to establish the science
of taxonomy, and its strange
animals threatened to derail
the whole project. Could the
kangaroo really fit into the
Linnaean category of the
Mammalia? Was the platypus
even, perhaps, a hoax – a duck's
head sewn onto the body of
something furry?

Kangaroo and other quadrupeds.
Friedrich Johann Justin Bertuch,
*Bilderbuch für Kinder, enthaltend eine
angenehme Sammlung von Thieren,
Pflanzen, Blumen, Früchten,
Mineralien, Trachten und allerhand
andern unterrichtenden Gegenständen
aus dem Reiche der Natur, der Künste
und Wissenschaften ...,*
Weimar, 1792–1830

In 1770, Cook's ship HMS *Endeavour*
hit a reef off Queensland, Australia and
the crew were forced to go ashore to
find food. They returned reporting a
creature as large as a greyhound, of a
mouse colour, and very swift. After its
preparation by the ship's cook, all agreed
that the kangaroo was excellent eating.

Australian wombat.
Watercolour by an unknown artist, inscribed '*From New Holland ... From a live specimen in the possession of Marquis Wellesley*'. Marquess Wellesley Collection of Natural History Drawings

The East India Company sponsored natural-historical research and pictorial documentation, mostly of plants, in the hopes that this knowledge might be commercially useful. Its governors and employees were often also natural historians in their own right, such as the Marquess of Wellesley, who assembled over 2,500 painted miniatures, not counting those he collected from further afield, such as this one.

Platypus
('*Ornithorhynchus paradoxus*').
Transactions of the Zoological Society, Vol. 1. Pl. 34, 1835

This scientific article gives an unexpectedly charming view of the platypus in several poses of rolling. 'When I held the unfortunate Platypus in my hands,' the article reported, 'its bright little eyes glistened, and the orifices of the ears were expanded and contracted alternately, as if eager to catch the slightest sound, while its heart palpitated violently with fear and anxiety. After it had been retained in the hands for some time [it] lost its first fear.'

OPPOSITE
Koalas.
Watercolour by unknown artist, inscribed on the back '*Coola, an animal of the opossum tribe from New South Wales*'. Marquess Wellesley Collection of Natural History Drawings

A report in the *Philosophical Transactions* of 1808 announced a new creature, seen a few years previously and known locally as a koala wombat. 'The ears are short, erect, and pointed; the eyes generally ruminating, sometimes fiery and menacing; it bears no small resemblance to the bear in the fore-part of its body.'

Ornithorhynchus paradoxus

C. R. Riley del.   J. Fittler sculp.

PINGUINARIA PATACHONICA.   THE PENGUIN.

Published as the Act directs July 2.1792.by I.Parkinson Leverian Museum.

King penguin ('*Pinguinaria patachonica*'). George Shaw, *Musei Leveriani explicatio Anglica et Latina (containing select specimens from the museum of the late Sir Ashton Lever, Kt., with descriptions in Latin and English),* London, 1792

The renowned explorer and naturalist Joseph Banks, on encountering penguins, noted with curiosity that their wings 'might ... almost as properly be call'd fins'. His correspondent Thomas Pennant begged Banks to send one of his penguin pictures to his sisters, perhaps inaugurating our tendency to see this most anthropomorphic of birds as, in Pablo Neruda's phrase, 'exemplary'.

'Sea Elephant (female). Drawn from Nature and on Stone by Waterhouse Hawkins'. John Richardson and John Edward Gray, *The Zoology of the Voyage of H.M.S. Erebus and Terror, under the Command of Capt. Sir James Clark Ross During the Years 1839 to 1843*, London 1844–75

Richardson and Gray were pleased to offer information on this little-known creature. Seals were regarded as difficult to study – different species were similar in form and appearance, and it was not easy to get close to them on their lonely, rocky shores.

Dugong.
Bijdragen tot de dierkunde ('Contributions to Zoology'), Amsterdam, 1848

Widely distributed in coastal waters from the Indian Ocean to the western Pacific, dugongs are commonly thought of as the origin of mermaid myths. However, honest scrutiny tends to correct this universally known factoid. Any sailor mistaking a dugong for a beautiful woman had been at sea for far too long.

'*The Polar Bear*'.
Number 11 in the Royal School
Series of Wall Pictures, late
nineteenth century

Hair-raising tales of attacks by the
ferocious white bear sealed the
scientific value of early-nineteenth-
century polar expeditions into a
narrative of adventure and conquest.

THE POLAR BEAR.

(No. II.—"Royal School Series" of Wall Pictures.)

'The Shark and Remora'.
John Gabriel Stedman,
*Narrative of a Five Years Expedition
against the Revolted Negroes of Surinam,
from the Year 1772 to 1777, Elucidating
the History of that Country
and Describing its Productions*,
London, 1796

Stedman's graphic and distressing tirade
against the evils of New World slavery
was leavened by sketches of native
wildlife. Stedman noted that the remora
used its sucker to fasten itself to ships,
with such force that 'no waves, however
violent, can beat it off'.

Ganges river dolphin.
Hand-coloured copperplate, drawn and
engraved by Richard Polydore Nodder,
from George Shaw,
The Naturalist's Miscellany,
London, 1789–1813

The wonderfully named Polydore
Nodders are examples of artists whose
lives have been lost to history, whilst
their collaborator in words – George
Shaw – remains reasonably well known.
Frederick Polydore Nodder contributed
illustrations to the first twelve volumes
of the *Miscellany*, and his son, Richard,
and wife, Elizabeth, continued the series
after his death in 1800. Elizabeth was,
needless to say, the least acknowledged
of the three.

Dolphin.
Pierre Belon,
De aquatilibus,
Paris, 1553

Belon's book on aquatic creatures included Conrad Gessner's monstrous monk fish (page 14), but elsewhere the Frenchman's natural history included such innovations as bone-by-bone comparisons of human and bird skeletons.

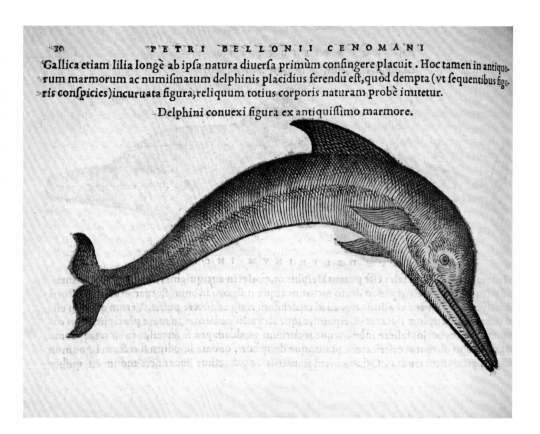

BALAENOPT

ANTARCTICA.

Sei whale ('*Balaenoptera antarctica*').
Philipp Franz von Siebold,
*Fauna Japonica sive descriptio animalium
quae in itinere per Japoniam*,
Leiden, 1833–50

This whale was doubly exotic, being from
Japan and rare even there. Siebold – somewhat
unusually for European naturalists – appears
to have taken local expertise seriously,
collaborating with Japanese naturalists as well
as employing them to collect specimens and
make drawings. He cites one such author in the
description of this whale, noting his belief that it
had been driven onto the shore whilst trying to
evade predation by killer whales.

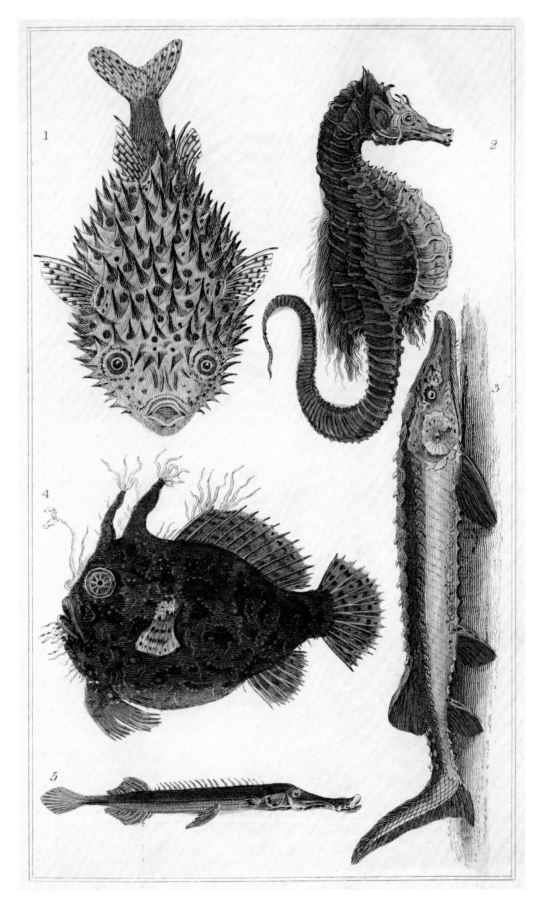

'*Sea porcupine,
hippocampus, sturgeon,
fishing frog* [sic],
pipe fish'.
Oliver Goldsmith,
*The History of the Earth
and Animated Nature*,
London, 1824

This book was perhaps a
surprising excursion for
a writer better known
as a novelist, poet, and
playwright. In her novel
The Mill on the Floss,
George Eliot had her
heroine Maggie Tulliver
describe its exotic
contents: '... elephants,
and kangaroos, and the
civet cat, and the sun-
fish, and a bird sitting
on its tail ... There are
countries full of those
creatures, instead of
horses and cows ...
Shouldn't you like to
know about them?'

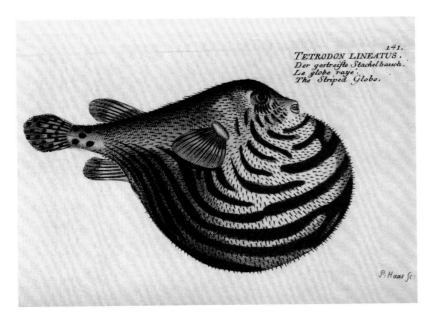

Striped globe fish ('*Tetrodon lineatus*').
Marcus Elieser Bloch,
Naturgeschichte des auslandische Fische,
Berlin 1786-7

Bloch was illiterate until relatively late in life,
when he stumbled into a medical education.
His life's work – twelve volumes on fish – was
divided into the domestic and the exotic. The
first three volumes dealt with German fish, while
the latter nine moved on to the more colourful
aquatic denizens of the rest of the world.

Puffer fish.
Albertus Seba,
*Locupletissimi rerum naturalium thesauri
accurata descriptio*,
Amsterdam, 1734–65

Seba's apothecary's shop near Amsterdam
harbour put him at the heart of the exotic animal
trade. He was able to inspect and sometimes
buy strange and fragile specimens such as this.

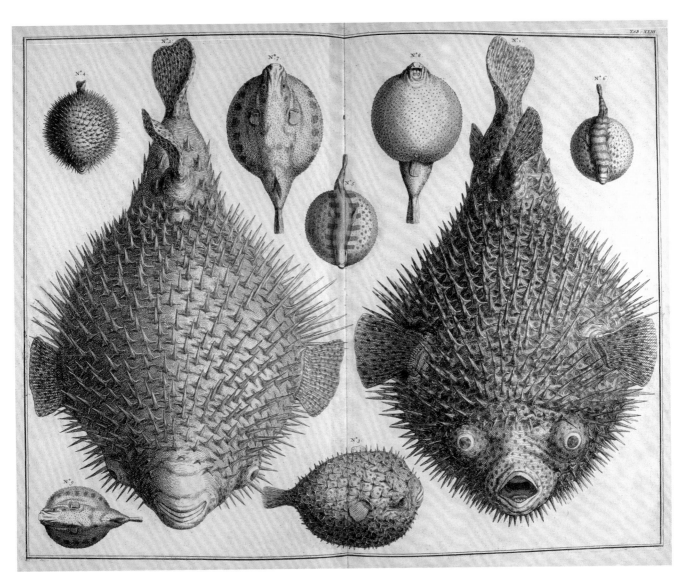

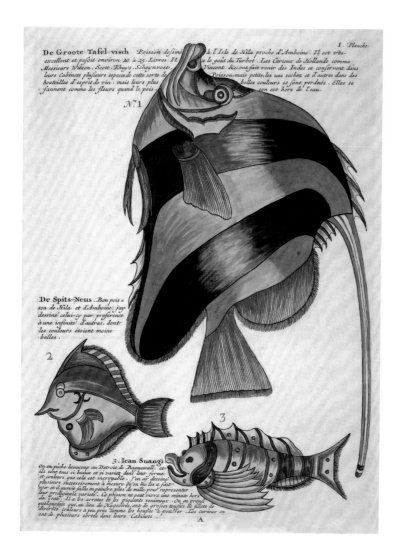

Bannerfish ('*De Groote Tafel-visch*') and others.
Louis Renard, 'Poissons, écrevisses et crabes ... que
l'on trouve autour des Isles Moluques, et sur les côtes
des Terres Australes' (manuscript of painted
drawings presented to Hans Sloane by Renard),
Amsterdam, early eighteenth century

Renard recommended the bannerfish (its label means
'Great Table Fish') as excellent eating, somewhere
close to a turbot in taste. The fish on the lower left
('*De Spits-Neus*') was also good on a plate, but the
'*Ican Suangi*' was noted instead for its colours, quite
incredible in their beauty and variety.

Cowfish ('*Tobin's Striped Trunk Fish*').
E. Donovan,
*The Naturalist's Repository,
or Monthly Miscellany of Exotic Natural History*,
London, 1823–8

This fish was first named by Shaw as 'Auritus', a
fanciful nod to the ear-like spines above its eyes.
Its human aspect is enhanced here in the head-on
presentation. Shaw also described the specimen –
collected by Cook – as deep brown; but this coloration
was due, as so often, to the poor conservation of the
fish once caught.

Expédition de F. de Castelnau.(Amérique du Sud).

7.e Partie. Zoologie. Poissons. Pl: 11.

1.ACANTHURUS BAHIANUS. Cast. 1.a. Ecailles Gr. Nat. 1.b. Ecailles grossies.

2.HOLACANTHUS FORMOSUS. Cast.

3.PLATAXOÏDES DUMERILII. Cast. 3.a.Bouche grossie. 3.b.Dents très-grossies.

Oudart Lith.   P.Bertrand éditeur.   Paris Lithographie Gény-Gros.

'*Acanthurus bahianus,
Holacanthus formosus,
Plataxoides dumerilii*'.
*Animaux nouveaux ou rares
recueillis pendant
L'Expedition dans les parties
centrales de l'Amerique du
Sud*, Vol. 7 (*Zoologies.
Mammifères*) in Count du
Castelnau, *Expedition dans
les parties centrales de
l'Amerique du Sud*, 1843

François Louis Nompar de
Caumont la Force, comte de
Castelnau, was sent on his
expedition by Louis Philippe I,
and was accompanied by two
botanists and a taxidermist.
Altogether they spent five
years roaming the continent
of South America.

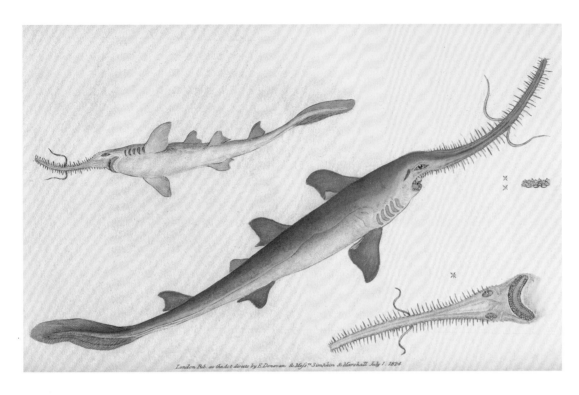

Tentaculated sawfish.
E. Donovan,
The Naturalist's Repository, or Monthly Miscellany of Exotic Natural History,
London 1823–8

The author asserts that, 'Our figure is copied from a very elegant and perfect specimen which was recently received from Van Dieman's [sic] Land.' The picture gives no room for doubt concerning the anatomical aspect which was of most interest in 'this curious species of the finny tribe'.

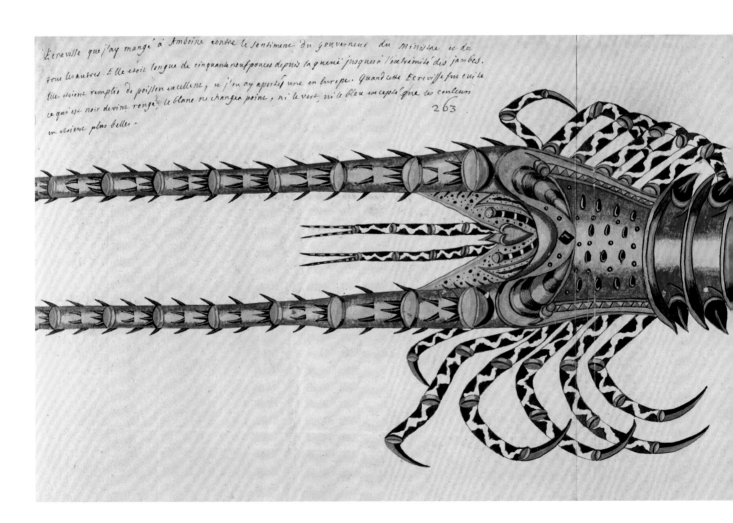

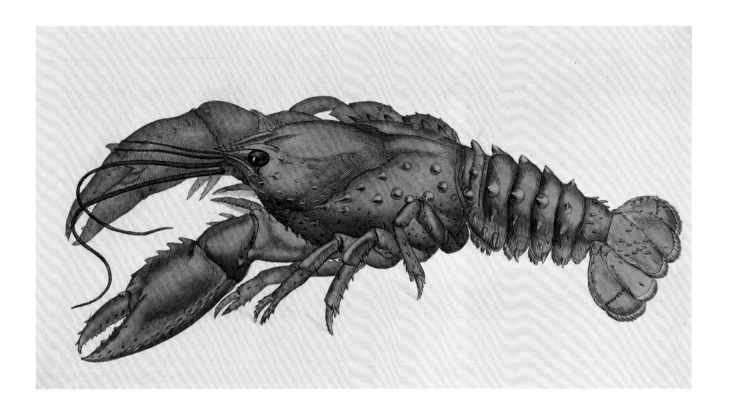

Serrated lobster.
George Shaw,
Zoology of New Holland,
London, 1794

The serrated lobster was the only invertebrate to be granted a place in Shaw's book. One of its 'curious' qualities is that in its coloration it resembles a ready-boiled lobster of the ordinary, edible kind.

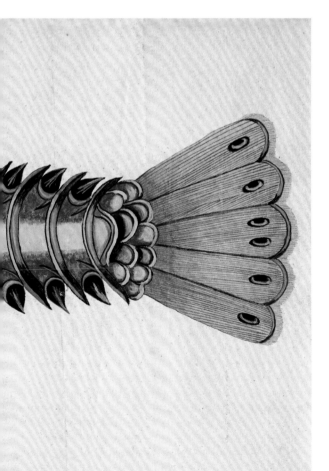

Crayfish ('*Ecrevisse que j'ay mangé à Amboine ...*').
Watercolour drawing for *Poissons, écrevisses et crabes: histoire naturelle des plus rares curiousitez de la Mer des Indes*, published by Louis Renard, 1718–19, and once owned by Hans Sloane

This creature is discussed principally for its gustatory qualities. The handwritten notes appear to indicate that the artist consumed it against the advice of several eminent persons. No harm, however, seems to have been done (except to the crayfish).

Crab ('*Cancer dentatus*').
Published in 'Observations on the Genus
Cancer of Dr. Leach with Descriptions
of three new species' by Thomas Bell,
from *Transactions of the
Zoological Society*,
London, 1835

Bell devoted his life to some of nature's less
glamorous creatures, amongst them the
Crustacea. In his *History of the British Stalk-
Eyed Crustacea*, he lamented that most
works of natural history lacked all but the
most superficial coverage of the class. This
beautifully textured illustration of an exotic
species helps to remedy that situation.

M. Gauci lithog.

Printed by C. Hullmandel.

Cancer dentatus.

10.

Coluber Porphyriacus.

Publish'd by J. Sowerby Sept.ʳ 10ᵗʰ 1794.

OPPOSITE
Red-bellied snake ('*Coluber Porphyriacus*').
George Shaw,
Zoology of New Holland,
London, 1794

From the first book of Australian animals –
indeed the first to establish 'Australia' as that
country's name – this snake finds a place
amongst many gorgeously coloured creatures.
The text notes: 'This beautiful snake ... appears
to be unprovided with tubular teeth or fangs,
and consequently not of a poisonous nature.'
The observation about beauty is indisputable,
but woe betide anyone taking the second part
as fact. The venom has neurotoxins, myotoxins,
coagulants, and haemolytic properties, and
anyone bitten requires immediate medical
attention.

SURINAAMSCHE RATEL~SLANG.

THE COBRA DE CAPELLO.

Surinamese rattlesnake.
Arnout Vosmaer,
*Description d'un recueil exquis d'animaux rares,
consistant en quadrupèdes, oiseaux et serpents,
des Indes Orientales et Occidentales ... Avec figures
dessinées et enluminées d'après nature*,
Amsterdam, 1804

'Some authors suppose,' commented Charles Darwin, 'that ... this
snake is furnished with a rattle for its own injury, namely, to warn
its prey to escape.' But Darwin would have none of it: 'I would
almost as soon believe that the cat curls the end of its tail when
preparing to spring, in order to warn the doomed mouse.'

Cobra.
James Forbes,
Oriental Memoirs,
London, 1813

Forbes noted in his *Memoirs* that
peacocks sometimes consume cobras,
even those of 'an almost incredible
magnitude'.

Chameleon forest dragon ('*Lophyrus tigrinus*'), a reptile native to Indonesia and Malaysia. Plate 1 from 'Descriptions de plusieurs espèces nouvelles du genre Lophyrus ... Mémoire accompané de trois Planches', by Hermann Schlegel, published in *Bijdragen tot de dierkunde* ('Contributions to Zoology'), Amsterdam, 1848–54

LOPHYRUS TIGRINUS

'*The Monitor Lizard*'.
Ebenezer Sibly,
*An Universal System of Natural History
Including the Natural History of Man, Etc.*,
London, 1794–1807

Joseph Banks honoured the lizard, a creature of many
and beautiful forms, with a place on his heraldic crest.
He explained, 'I have taken the Lizard, an Animal said
to be Endowed by nature with an instinctive Love of
mankind ... as a Perpetual Remembrance, that man is
never so well employed, as when he is Labouring for
the advantage of the public.'

A curiously spotted lizard dug out of a hillock close to Col. Salters tent near Moolton Oct. 1848. Copied from the drawing of Brigadier Salter C. B.

The natives (reports Brigadier Salter) say that it is a very uncommon reptile of the Biskhra species and not found in our provinces. Some officers mentioned that it is found in our provinces in humidity and its native name Zekoe.

Agra Oct 28. 1854.

Lizard.
Artist unknown.
Sheet dated '*Oct. 28 1854*'

Written on the sheet at top is 'Suspended in spirits', and below, 'a curiously spotted lizard dug out of a hillock close to Col. Salters tent near Modtan Oct. 1848. copied from the drawing of Brigadier Salter P.B.' The practice of transporting corpses in jars of rum often backfired; alas, this preservative often proved too tempting for the sailors *en route*, resulting in the destruction of the specimen.

Salamander.
George Shaw,
The Naturalist's Miscellany,
London, 1789–1813

The salamander was traditionally supposed to pass through fire without harm; Edward Topsell, however, was sceptical of Aristotle's claim. With a rhetorical flourish, he asked readers what they thought of the fact that the philosopher would 'write upon hear-say … and out of the same to furnish both the present and all future ages [with knowledge]'.

Horned frog.
George Shaw,
The Naturalist's Miscellany,
London, 1789–1813

The original text with this picture asks unkindly: 'Should inquiry be made, which is the ugliest animal yet known to exist? The creature here represented might perhaps with justice be proposed as an answer: an animal of such prodigious deformity as even to exceed in this respect the Surinam toad, or Rana Pipa.'

Rhinoceros beetles. 'A Book containing Severall sort of Insects from Europe, Asia, Africa etc. America: painted from the life in their naturall colours from the collection of Mr Albert Seba of Amsterdam' (manuscript collection), 1728

The largest rhinoceros beetles can grow to 17 centimetres (over 6 inches) in length. Gigantic insects eventually came to figure as nightmarish foes of humanity in the science-fictional imagination, thanks in no small part to H. G. Wells. In real life things went the other way; many species are now endangered, owing to collecting and loss of habitat.

Atlas beetle
('*Dynastes Chalcosoma Atlas*').
Edward Donovan,
Natural History of the Insects of India,
London, 1842

It is impossible to see a beetle picture like this without thinking of Dürer's lifelike insect, picking its way across the shadowed page.

BELOW LEFT
Pink-winged grasshopper.
'A Book containing Severall sort of Insects from Europe, Asia, Africa etc. America: painted from the life in their naturall colours from the collection of Mr Albert Seba of Amsterdam', 1728

Unlike the beetle or the locust, these grasshoppers are portrayed as specimens rather than living creatures. They form an organised pattern, beautiful in its own right.

BELOW RIGHT
Shock shock locust, female.
E. Donovan,
The Naturalist's Repository, or Monthly Miscellany of Exotic Natural History,
London, 1823–8

This locust is so named because of its call, resembling the words 'shock-shock' slowly and loudly repeated. Donovan says that the sounds made by the insect commence at sunset and are 'so loud that [they] may be heard at the distance of a mile from the spot where it lies concealed'.

Papilio Ulysses.

OPPOSITE
Butterfly ('*Papilio Ulysses*').
E. Donovan,
*The Naturalist's Repository, or Monthly
Miscellany of Exotic Natural History*,
London, 1823–8

Butterflies are very fragile, yet require
nothing by way of stuffing or preserving.
They were sometimes slipped between
the pages of a book like pressed flowers.
The oldest known specimens, exotic
trophies from around the world, are
around 300 years of age: an eternity
compared with their brief flash of life.

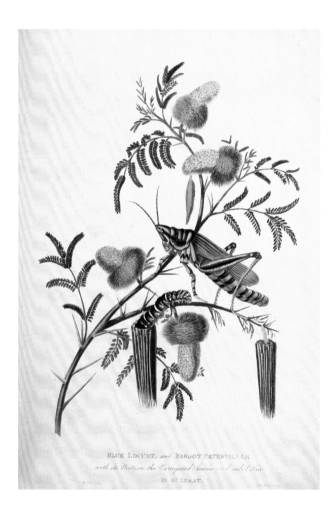

Butterfly.
John Obadiah Westwood,
*The Cabinet of Oriental Entomology, Being a Selection of
some of the Rarer and More Beautiful Species of Insects,
Natives of India and the Adjacent Islands*, London, 1848

Westwood's title indicates that his book fulfils, in paper
form, the function of the collector's cabinet. But it had an
additional, perhaps more surprising, aim: 'The present work
... is proposed to be ... a pictorial illustration of the larger and
more splendid species; and ... it is hoped, that, by finding
its way to the table of the Indian drawing-room, it may ...
awaken an interest in the objects of pursuit, thus supplying
an engaging occupation to our Indian friends.'

'*Blue Locust and Faggot Caterpillar, with its nest on the
Variegated Acacia or Baubal Tree in Guzerat*'.
James Forbes, *Oriental Memoirs*, London, 1813

James Forbes was appointed Collector of Bharuch in the late
1770s. There, he witnessed a flight of locusts 'extending above
a mile in length, and half as much in breadth ... like a black
cloud, [it] cast an awful gloom like that of an eclipse over the
garden, and caused a noise like the rushing of a torrent, they
were near on an hour in passing over our little territory'. Of the
faggot caterpillar he wrote, 'The baubul tree (Acacia) afforded
a curious specimen of insect sagacity in the Caterpillar's nests,
suspended by thousands to the branches. This little animal,
conscious of its approaching change ... instinctively provides
itself a strong mansion during that metamorphosis.'

Moths.

Watercolours, from 'A Book containing Severall sort of Insects from Europe, Asia, Africa etc. America: painted from the life in their naturall colours from the collection of Mr Albert Seba of Amsterdam', (manuscript collection), 1728

Seba opportunistically sold his first collection to Peter the Great in 1715, then began collecting all over again. This time, he recorded it permanently, hiring thirteen artists to draw the pictures that were printed in the four-volume *Thesaurus*, published over thirty years. When confronted with an animal he did not know, he simply made up a name.

OPPOSITE
Spiders.
Maria Sybilla Merian,
Metamorphosis insectorum Surinamensium,
Amsterdam, 1705

Top left is the huntsman spider (*Heteropoda venatoria*) while the two large, foreground specimens are pinktoe tarantulas (*Avicularia avicularia*). The German word for tarantula, *Vogelspinne*, translates literally as 'bird spider'— and this engraving may well be the origin of that word. Created from sketches drawn in Surinam, it shows a large spider that has captured a bird (left). Army ants (attacking a spider) and leaf-cutters are also shown in this exotic cornucopia of invertebrates.

Delalande's H.Bird.
T. Delalandii.
Brasil.
22

Mango Humming Bird
Young
27

LEFT
Red bird of paradise ('*L'Oiseau de Paradis rouge*').

BELOW
Nebuleux bird of paradise ('*Le Nebuleux*'), named by Le Vaillant for its 'cloud of white feathers'. Both from François Le Vaillant, *Histoire naturelle des Oiseaux de Paradis et des Rollers, suivie de celle des Toucans et des Barbus*, Paris, 1806

RIGHT
Greater bird of paradise
('*Paradisea apoda*').

BELOW
Magnificent bird of paradise
('*Diphyllodes speciosa*').
Both from John Gould,
*The Birds of New Guinea and
the Adjacent Papuan Islands,
Including any New Species that
may be Discovered in Australia,*
London, 1875

PARADISEA APODA. Lyn.

DIPHYLLODES SPECIOSA.

In May 1862, Alfred Russel Wallace described to the Zoological Society of London his incredible adventures in search of birds of paradise. He suffered attack by pirates; members of his party died of dysentery and got swept away to uninhabited desert islands. His misfortunes – or those of his fellow-travellers – enhanced the value of his finds: 'Nature seems to have taken every precaution that these, her choicest treasures, may not lose value by being too easily obtained.'

Darwin observed in *The Descent of Man* (1871) that birds of paradise exhibit the most extreme sexual dimorphism known amongst the class Aves. 'Female birds of paradise are obscurely coloured and destitute of all ornaments, whilst the males are probably the most highly decorated of all birds, and in so many different ways that they must be seen to be appreciated.' They formed a crucial example of an evolutionary mechanism supplementary to natural selection: sexual selection. Females selected arbitrary forms of 'beauty' in potential mates, thereby ensuring the continuation and exaggeration of the traits down the generations, in the absence of (or even contrary to) their survival value. Darwin noted, with unintentional poignancy:

'With birds of paradise a dozen or more full-plumaged males congregate in a tree to hold a dancing-party ... and the whole tree seems, as Mr. Wallace remarks, to be filled with waving plumes. When thus engaged, they become so absorbed that a skilful archer may shoot nearly the whole party.'

Le Toco. N.º 2.

Barraband f.

Pérée sculp.

Toucan ('*Le Toco, No. 2*')
François Le Vaillant,
*Histoire naturelle des Oiseaux de
Paradis et des Rollers, suivie de celle
des Toucans et des Barbus*, Paris, 1806

Le Vaillant noted in his description how
difficult it was to preserve the bold
colours of the toucan's beak after death.
Le Vaillant was, indeed, a pioneer in the
use of colour in scientific illustration.

Ground parrot ('*Psittacus terrestris*').
George Shaw,
Zoology of New Holland,
London, 1794

The vivacity of Sowerby's engravings
for Shaw is remarkable, given that he
was working from skins, skeletons,
and pickled specimens shipped all
the way from Australia.

Ultramarine lorikeet.
Richard Brinsley Hinds,
*The Zoology of the Voyage of H.M.S. Sulphur
under the Command of Captain Sir E. Belcher*
(section on birds by J. Gould),
London, 1843–5

Exotic bird plumage in millinery became a
fatal craze amongst wealthy women of the
late nineteenth century, on both sides of
the Atlantic; once again exotica in science
mingled with trade and exploitation of
the natural and human worlds.

ABOVE
Parakeet.
Inscribed on plate: '*from the Spice Islands
of the bignes of a Good hen*'.

RIGHT
Parrot.
Inscribed on plate: '*somewhat less than Life*'.
Added in pencil: '*Psittacus Edwards*'.
Original watercolours of birds by George Edwards,
first half of the eighteenth century

Edwards was financially liberated to pursue his art by his powerful patron,
the collector Hans Sloane, who secured him an undemanding job at the Royal
College of Physicians. Edwards established global connections with many
naturalists, and was taught the art of engraving by Mark Catesby. Together
these factors enabled him to become a successful producer of books.

somewhat less than Life.

Edwards

Native

Just as it takes a journey abroad to make one see the quirks of one's own homeland afresh, so it took the exploration of distant lands, and the recording of their exotic beasts, to bring Europeans an awareness of the fauna that was native to their homes. Before that, the animals they saw were simply all the animals that there were; they filled out the category of 'animals' in its entirety.

Having got a taste for recording and identifying creatures abroad, naturalists turned their attention to their own faunas. Europeans and Americans became interested in the visual documentation of their native creatures, particularly in the nineteenth century. There was, perhaps, a frisson of scientific pleasure in seeing one's own natural history through de-familiarised eyes. There was also a possibility, for some kinds of animal at least, of achieving a completeness of recording. Drawing all the mammals, or even all the butterflies, of England seemed like an achievable task. Adding to the catalogue, or correcting it, was a pleasurably useful and expert activity.

Native drawing and recording also gave the opportunity to study natural history to those who did not have the money to sponsor foreign travel, or who could not (or would not) find a patron to pay for their own. Recording native fauna was part of a general trend in natural philosophy and natural history; by the nineteenth century, these activities had made their way down through the social strata, so that middle-class expertise could now trump gentlemanly authority.

The nineteenth-century expansion of reading, railways, and leisure time all helped to create a readership hungry for images of creatures that they themselves might hope to see. In the United States particularly, an emergent sense of national identity was underpinned by a proud identification of the animals and birds that made the continent exceptional. Later on, fears about industrialisation and modernity in both the United States and the United Kingdom fed a hunger for the idyllic landscape of times past, its native fauna still-living signifiers of an unfallen nature, untouched by humankind.

The awareness of a native fauna also tracked, historically, the growth of the nation state and of nationalism. There is no 'native' unless there is a humanly defined state to contain it, and these states emerged, broadly speaking, during the modern period. The rigidity of scientific classificatory schemes – for which that of Linnaeus was the model – echoed the increasing comprehensiveness with which human subjects, or citizens, were recorded and manipulated by emergent European states. Systems of taxation, of conscription, of voting, policing, and census-taking all mirrored the ordering of the natural world. Indeed, recording all the fauna within

'*Peacock butterfly on Smith's Newington Peach*'.
Benjamin Wilkes,
The English Moths and Butterflies, Together with the Plants, Flowers and Fruits, Whereon They Feed, and Are Usually Found,
London 1747–60

Benjamin Wilkes apparently began painting butterflies as a means to improve his portraiture, but became increasingly fascinated by – and knowledgeable concerning – the Lepidoptera. His first book of illustrations assembled them in simple patterns, but here he attempts to show the 'plants, flowers, and fruits, whereon they feed, and are usually found', along with 'an attempt towards a [life-]history'. The image-heavy book was a luxury product, and in today's terms would cost around £1,500.

Bald eagle.
Drawing by George Edwards
after Mark Catesby.
First half of the eighteenth century

Benjamin Franklin, one of the founding
fathers of the United States, objected
to the adoption of the bald eagle as
the American national symbol on the
grounds that it was 'a Bird of bad moral
Character ... generally poor and often
very lousy ... a rank Coward'.

a state's boundaries was another way of defining its borders, and inscribing its legitimacy upon nature.

If fish were an early group to satisfy the thirst for drawings of animal exotica, so birds were an early – and long-lasting – visual epitome of native faunas. The *Birds of Britain* (and sundry, closely-allied titles) is probably the most over-used book name in the whole of natural history. The reason for birds' popularity as fulfilment of the native-animal category is hard to fathom completely. Perhaps there is something intrinsically compelling about their ability to live in another realm, the airy sky. But then fish, too, live in another element from ours. Birds, however, unlike fish, can exist in human space; they are not compelled to live apart from us, but choose to touch down upon the Earth before flying once again upwards. Perhaps they still speak to the medieval Christian cosmos so deeply engrained in European cultures, mediating between the celestial realm and our own Earthbound existence.

Birds are also, as it happens, the most popular choice of animal for national symbols, bringing together native natural history and the birth of the state. These symbols are very often eagles, a proud and forceful image for a nation. Upon declaring independence, a committee of Americans immediately declared the golden eagle as the new nation's symbol, but a few years later switched to the more geographically specific – and hugely memorable – bald eagle. The United Kingdom, curiously, has never had an official national bird, perhaps because its more dramatic predator species tend to be found in the (relatively) recently and controversially annexed Scotland. An unofficial vote conducted in 2015 selected the European robin as the people's choice, a less politically assertive species than the raptors of the nineteenth century. It was a bird for a post-colonial, sentimental world.

'*The Ancient Wrasse*'.
Philip Henry Gosse,
*The Aquarium: An Unveiling
of the Wonders of the Deep Sea*,
London, 1854

Philip Gosse's 'Ancient Wrasse'
(now known as the Ballan wrasse)
would have been a lucky find for a
Victorian naturalist, as these fish swim
a good deal deeper than paddling
depth. Its inclusion in a book of
natural history indicates that the
collection of animal images was
almost a hobby in its own right.

P.H.Gosse, del.

Hanhart Chromo lith.

43. Roach. Nail size.

S. Brodick del.

Carp ('*Cyprinus Carpio*').
Hand-coloured engraved plate by F. Assner
from Baron Carl von Meidinger,
Icones piscium Austriae indigenorum,
Vienna, 1785–94

In many eastern European countries, the carp is traditional fare
for Christmas dinner, and may even swim for a day or two in
the family bath-tub before being killed and eaten.

Cyprinus Carpio. LINN.

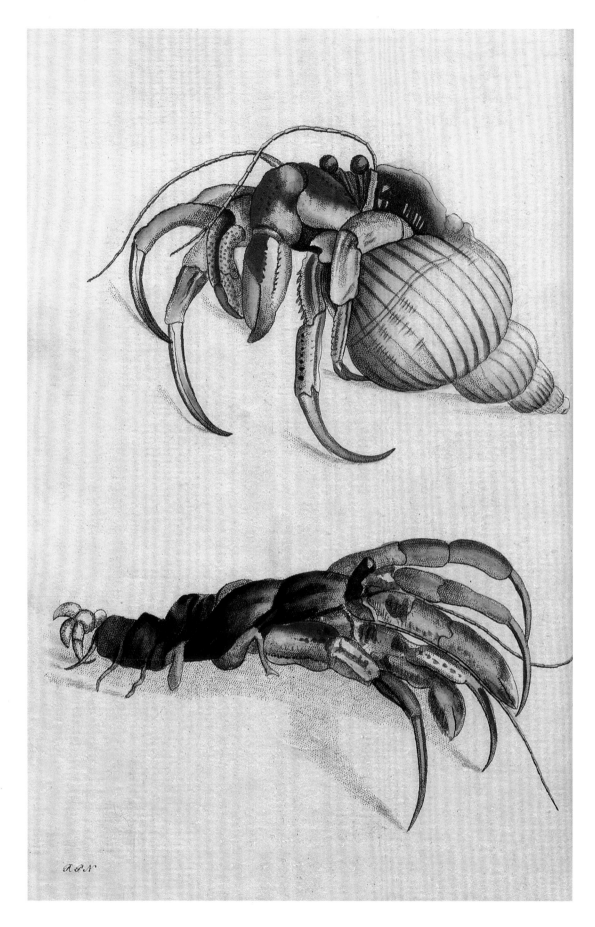

George Eliot's lover, the critic
G. H. Lewes, collected two
hermit crabs from the seaside.
He took them home and, as was
the nineteenth-century fashion,
placed them in a marine aquarium.
Naming them after two famous
actors of the day, he removed
one of their shells and made the
pair compete for the one that
remained.

Crab ('*De Hirsutis Cancris, Rondeletius*').
Conrad Gessner,
Historiae animalium, Tiguri, 1551–8

The original watercolour by Cornelius Sittardus, after which
this engraving was made, is very different from another of
the same period by Guillaume Rondelet, also labelled as
the *Cancer hirsutus*, and recently identified as the warty
crab, *Eriphia verrucosa*. Sittardus' watercolour, it has
been suggested, may show what is now known as *Dromia
personata*, which has a velvety texture thanks to its copious
short hairs. However, *Dromia* has very fat claws, which the
main drawing at least does not appear to show.

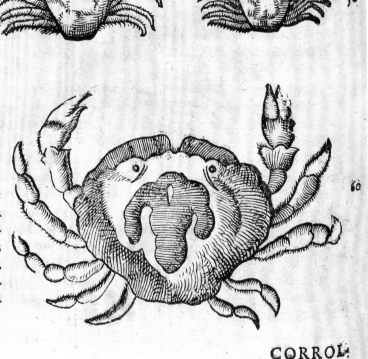

DE HIRSVTIS CANCRIS, RONDELETIVS.

Hirfuta funt quædam concrorum genera, variis in partibus, alia in fupina
parte, alia in pedibus.

Paruorum vero cancrorū qui hirfuti funt,
differentias tres obferuaui. Prima eft eorum
qui chelas aculeatas habent, & in extremo
nigrefcentes. Cornicula duo: quæ fequuntur
vtrinque partes, feratæ funt. In tefta media
cordis humani figura expreffa cernitur. Che-
lis pedibufque omnibus hirtis funt.

2   Huic generi fimile aliud eft æque hirfu-
tum, fed magnitudine differt. minus enim eft
fuperiore, & chelarum extrema nigricantia
non habet.

3   Tertia differentia eorum eft, qui fecundis
ita fimiles funt, vt eofdem cum iis plane effe
diceres, dempta fola magnitudine: nifi oua in
vtrifq; reperiffem: quod facit vt credam fpe-
cie differre, tamen, ob magnam cum fecundis
affinitaté, pictura horū feparata nil opus fuit.

C   Tria hæc genera cum reliquis pifcibus e-
uerruntur, & ob exiguitatem prorfus negli-
guntur.

CORROL:

Atlantic Right Whale.

Humpbacked Whale.

$\frac{1}{75}$

OPPOSITE
'*Atlantic Right Whale.
Humpbacked Whale*'.
Archibald Thorburn,
British Mammals,
London, 1920

Including deep-sea mammals in
a national collection is a powerful
statement; at the time, territorial waters
were considered to extend only three
nautical miles, whereas whales are often
further out. Today, whaling continues
to be mixed in with the politics of
maritime control.

Seal.
Thomas Pennant,
The British Zoology,
London, 1766

Pennant naturalised the seal to his native
Wales by giving the Celtic name: 'Moelrhon
from the word Moel, bald, or without ears,
and Rhon, a spear or lance'.

Otter.

Beaver.
Conrad Gessner,
Historiae animalium, Tiguri, 1551–8

The beaver's thick, waterproof fur
and its musk (used for medicine)
caused it to be hunted to extinction
in Britain in the sixteenth century. It
was reintroduced to Scotland in 2009,
though not without controversy. Land-
owners feared destruction of trees and
flooding due to the beavers' river-
damming activities.

Skunk ('*Pseudo phalangium*').
Mark Catesby,
*The Natural History of Carolina,
Florida and the Bahama Islands*,
London, 1731–43

Catesby notes, 'From some secret duct, it emits such fetid effluviums, that the atmosphere for a large space round shall be so infected with them, that men and other animals are impatient till they are quit of it ... The Indians, notwithstanding, esteem their flesh a dainty, of which I have eat, and found it well tasted.'

Black squirrel.
Mark Catesby,
*The Natural History of Carolina,
Florida and the Bahama Islands*,
London, 1731–43

Catesby was at first unsure whether or not these squirrels were the same species as the grey kind. Eventually, after some time spent in observing them, he concluded that due to their manner of 'breeding, associating, and other circumstances', they were indeed unique.

OPPOSITE
'*Otter*'.
Archibald Thorburn,
British Mammals, London, 1920

Otters declined perilously in Britain in the decades following the 1950s, mainly due to poisoning by agricultural pesticides. New legislation has seen their numbers increase again since the 1990s, and in 2011 the Environment Agency announced they had returned to almost every county in the land.

CASSELL'S NATURAL HISTORY WALL SHEETS.

THE WILD BOAR. *(Sus Scrofa.)*

'*The Wild Boar (Sus Scrofa)*'.
Drawing by Friedrich Specht
for No. 4 in Cassell's Natural History
Wall Sheets, late nineteenth century

The naturalist Thomas Bell's observation (1837) that the wild boar 'infests many parts of Europe' leads us to surmise that he wasted no tears on the medieval extinction of the creature in Britain. This visual representation (by Friedrich Specht) from later in the century does not exactly salvage its reputation.

Fallow deer buck (stag).
Edward Topsell,
The History of Four-footed Beasts and Serpents
(single-volume edition),
London, 1658

Topsell informs his readers that the fallow deer is familiarly known as the 'palmed hart' for the finger-like projections of its 'horns'.

C.R.Ryley del.t   W.Skelton Sculp.t

Wolf.
George Shaw,
Musei Leveriani explicatio, Anglica et Latina
(containing select specimens from the museum
of the late Sir Ashton Lever, Kt., with descriptions
in Latin and English), London, 1792

According to some sources, this squinty-eyed,
doggy-looking wolf is actually the last of its kind shot
in Britain. Unfortunately, like fishermen's tales, stories
of the shooting of the last wolf abound and none has
been definitively authenticated so far. Some sense
of the Victorian fascination with such animals, and
their histories, can be gained from James Edmund
Harting's *British Animals Extinct within Historic Times*.

Pine marten ('*The Marten*').
Thomas Pennant,
The British Zoology,
London, 1766

Pine martens were native to the remoter parts of
the British Isles; Pennant identified them as identical
to their North American cousins, now known as a
separate species. Pennant remarked on the saleability
of the latter's skins: up to 30,000 were exported
annually from Canada to France alone.

BELOW
'*The Badger*'.
William MacGillivray,
*A History of British
Quadrupeds*, Vol. 13 in
Jardine's The Naturalist's
Library, London, 1843

MacGillivray states that the
badger is 'extremely rare'
in most parts of Britain;
presumably this was due to
the popular working-class
entertainments of badger-
hunting and badger-baiting
with dogs. The latter was
outlawed in 1835, and the
badger population was
perhaps beginning to
rebound at the time of
this book's publication.

THE BADGER.

OPPOSITE
Hare.
Eleanor Edith Helme,
The Book of Birds and Beasties …
Paintings by Barbara Briggs,
London, 1929

The sentimental title of this book accords with the tone of the visual rendering. This hare is almost like a rabbit, and its character looks far from the coltish, boxing madness of other cultural representations.

Harvest mouse.
Edward Donovan,
The Natural History of British Quadrupeds,
London, 1820

Perhaps the most beloved of the family Muridae, this beautiful little auburn mouse never invades human spaces, but remains in the field – where it is tragically susceptible to destruction during harvest season.

'*The Hedgehog*'.
Thomas Pennant,
The British Zoology,
London, 1766

'It lies under the undeserved reproach of sucking cattle, and hurting their udders,' Pennant tells us, 'but the smallness of its mouth renders that impossible.'

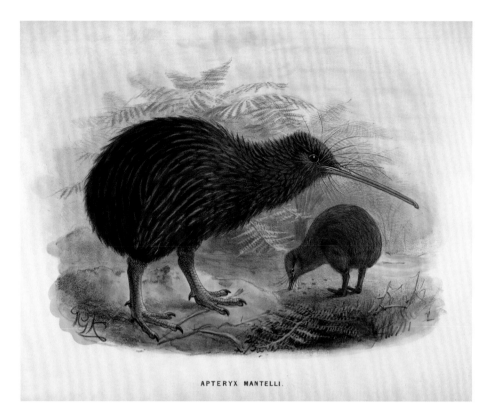

APTERYX MANTELLI.

As colonial confidence grew,
so books appeared that
celebrated and implicitly
claimed the native fauna
of new landscapes.

Laughing kookaburra
('*Dacelo gigantea*').
John Gould,
The Birds of Australia,
London, 1848–69

The French naturalist Pierre
Sonnerat published the first
description of this species in
1776, implying that he had
observed it in New Guinea
– an impossibility. It seems
likely that a specimen was
collected by Joseph Banks
and a colleague, and given to
Sonnerat by Banks when
they crossed paths at the
Cape of Good Hope in 1770.
The species is now known as
the kookaburra, its name in
the Wiradhuri language.

BACON'S CHART OF BRITISH BIRDS

COLOURED FAITHFULLY FROM NATURE

INCLUDING

THE PRINCIPAL VARIETIES OF BIRDS FOUND IN THE UNITED KINGDOM,

WITH ILLUSTRATIONS OF THE CHIEF SPECIES OF BIRDS OF PREY, GAME-BIRDS, SONG-BIRDS, WATER-BIRDS, AND MIGRATORY-BIRDS;

PECULIAR TO GREAT BRITAIN AND IRELAND;

The name of every bird represented in this Chart will be found in the accompanying letterpress. Where two or more Birds are represented in one illustration, the names are given in order from left to right.

Juvenal's expression of implausibility, *rara
avis in terris nigroque simillima* ('a rare
bird in the earth and most similar to a
black swan'), was widely quoted in early-
modern England. The discovery in 1697
that such a bird really existed in Australia
at once provided a meme for philosophical
rumination and a confirmation of the topsy-
turvy nature of the southern hemisphere.
The bird was proudly adopted as a symbol
of Australian-ness by the state of
Western Australia in 1870.

Owls ('*Sirix Bubo,
The Great Eagle Owle; Otus
sive Asio, the Horn-Owle;
Scops Aldrow, the little
Horn Owle*').
Francis Willughby,
The Ornithology of F. W.,
London, 1678

This volume is thought to be one
of the first attempts to classify
birds systematically. Willughby's
horned owl seems to be what
is now known as a Eurasian
eagle-owl, and his claim to have
located one in Yorkshire seems
implausible. His contact, one
Francis Jessop, must have had
it from the continent.

OPPOSITE
Snowy owl.
Chromolithograph by
J. G. Keulemans from
Johann Naumann,
*Naturgeschichte der Vögel
Mittel-Europas*,
Gera-Untermhaus, 1905

The snowy owl, which
occasionally (though
increasingly rarely) ventures as
far south as Scotland, has been
used as a characteristic national
fauna, in contradistinction to
that of England.

Cormorant ('*Pelecanus Carbo*').
Cornelius Nozeman,
Nederlandsche Vogelen,
Amsterdam, 1770–1829

Two generations of artists were involved in this mammoth
production, which took almost sixty years to complete. They
promised that the illustrations were *naer het leven* ('from the
life'), and to emphasise their skill often presented a *trompe l'œil*
picture-within-a-picture, as in this example, thus by implication
elevating the main engraving to the status of life itself.

OPPOSITE
Pelican.
John J. Audubon,
Birds of America,
London, 1827–38

For some reason birds do
most service amongst the
animal kingdom as national
emblems, and almost any one
of Audubon's magnificent
specimens could do as insignia
for his native America. This
pelican stands proud, almost
bursting beyond the bounds
of its darkly majestic frame.

PELECANUS Carbo.

OPPOSITE
Common heron
('*Ardea Major*').
George Graves,
British Ornithology,
London, 1811–21
Graves promised
the satisfaction of
completeness, with
every known species of
British bird included in
his three volumes.

'*Great Crested Grebe. 1 Adult
2 Young after 2nd moult*'.
Prideaux John Selby,
Atlas [Illustrations of British
Ornithology],
Edinburgh, 1825–33

William Swainson considered
this collection of 222 plates 'the
most splendid and costly work yet
published on the birds of Great
Britain'. Many of Selby's pictures
contain little by way of background
or additional decoration, in contrast
to the fuller, busier, and prettier
pictures of the high Victorian period.

GREAT CRESTED GREBE.
1 Adult. 2 Young after 2ᵈ moult.

PLATE LXXIII.

Ardea Major.

Pub. by G. Graves, Walworth. 1. Feb. 1811.

Title page, Eugenio Bettoni,
*Storia naturale degli uccelli che nidificano
in Lombardia* ('Natural History of the
Birds of Lombardy'),
Milan, 1865–71

Austria ceded Lombardy to Napoleon III in
1859, at which point it was annexed to the
nascent Italian state, a process completed
in 1866. This book therefore naturalises and
vindicates the historic boundaries of the
kingdom of Lombardy during a period of
state change.

'*The Bittern*'.
Thomas Pennant,
The British Zoology,
London, 1766

Thomas Bewick, who published his own
volumes on British quadrupeds and
birds some thirty years after Pennant,
gives several traditional English names
for this marsh-dwelling, booming bird:
bog-bumper, bitter-bum, mire-drum.

Crimson rocella parrot ('*Platycercus adelaidiæ*'). John Gould, *The Birds of Australia*, London, 1848–69

Like many Australian species (such as the kookaburra), the crimson rocella parrot has been introduced to nearby lands, in this case to New Zealand and Norfolk Island. These acts speak of a sense of ownership of both land and fauna: a sense of defining what is native.

PLATYCERCUS ADELAIDIÆ: *Gould*

Rock thrush
('*Petrocincla saxatilis*').
John Gould,
The Birds of Great Britain,
London, 1873

This was an optimistic
inclusion amongst native
species, as it is a rare visitor
to northern Europe. It
breeds in southern Europe
and through central Asia,
wintering in sub-Saharan
Africa.

PETROCINCLA SAXATILIS.

GRAESSNER, VOGELEIER.

X.

1. Anser cinereus. 2. Anas penelope. 3. Anas acuta. 4. Eudytes septentrionalis. 5. Lestris catarrhactes. 6. Lestris parasitica. 7. Platalea leucorodia. 8. Ardea cinerea. 9. Ardea purpurea. 10, a. b. Phalaropus cinereus. 11. Merops apiaster. 12. Picus canus. 13, a. b. c. d. Turdus pilaris. 14. Cinclus aquaticus. 15, a. b. c. d. Lanius collurio. 16, a. b. Salicaria locustella.

Birds' eggs
('*1. Anser cinereus.* [etc.]').
Johann Friedrich Naumann,
*Die Vogel von Mittel-
Europa*, Dresden, 1880–1

Collecting birds' nests and eggs was a (destructive) craze of the nineteenth and twentieth centuries. The hobby had the advantage that the specimens could be brought home to be checked against illustrations in a book: such spotter's guides did not have to be taken into the field, and so, in the nineteenth century at least, could be high-end publications.

BELOW LEFT
'Nest and egg of a Reed Warbler'.

BELOW RIGHT
'Nest and egg of a Wren'.
Both from F. O. Morris,
*A Natural History of the Nests
and Eggs of British Birds,*
London, 1853–6

Morris was a keen collector of birds and
insects in boyhood, and as an adult (by
which time he was a country parson) he
wrote prolifically on natural history for
children and adults. Ironically, his
book on nests and eggs – implicitly
encouraging their collection – probably
worked against his later-life commitment
to bird protectionism.

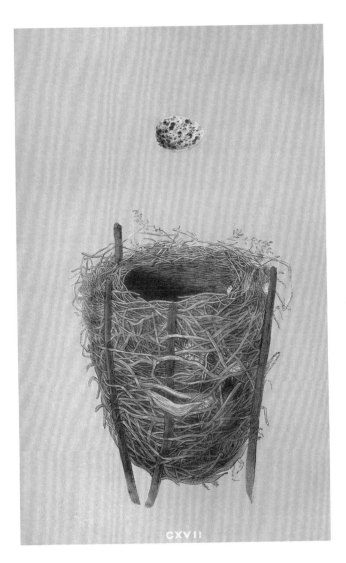

A. Thorburn. 1915.

Capercaillie (♂♀)

Capercaillie.
Archibald Thorburn,
British Birds,
London, 1915–18

Archibald Thorburn, though trained and living in London, based some of his most splendid paintings on birds characteristic of his native Scotland. Thorburn's paintings were re-used shortly after his death to illustrate the *Observer's Book of British Birds* (the first of the Observer's guides).

BELOW
'Redwing' and 'Cuckoo'.
Thomas Bewick,
A General History of Birds and Quadrupeds,
Philadelphia, 1824.

'Summer is icumen in' (late thirteenth century) is the oldest-known musical round with English words. Its lyrics culminate with triumphant onomatopoeic repetition of that best-loved sound of the English summer:

Murie sing cuccu
Cuccu cuccu
Wel singes þu cuccu
ne swik þu nauer nu
Sing cuccu nu Sing cuccu.
Sing cuccu Sing cuccu nu

Starling
('*Sturnis volugaris, Linn.,*
Winter').
Plate by John Garard Keulemans from Thomas Littleton Powys Lilford, (Baron), *Coloured Figures of the Birds of the British Islands*, London, 1885–97

The common starling is a cosmopolitan bird, native across Europe and Asia and successfully settled as far afield as Australia, the Americas North and South, the Falkland Islands, South Africa, and Fiji.

STARLING.
Sturnus vulgaris, *Linn.*
Winter.

REDWING.

CUCKOO.

Cayenne tern (with crab).
John J. Audubon,
Birds of America,
London, 1827–38

The cayenne tern (*Thalasseus eurygnatha*) has
recently had doubt cast upon its species status;
it is very similar to, and intergrades with,
populations of Cabot's tern (*T. acuflavidus*).
Throughout the period covered by this book,
species were constantly being created and
discarded in this fashion.

EUDYPTES CHRYSOCOMUS.   EUDYPTULA MINOR.

PUFFIN.
Fratacula artica *(Linn.)*

Southern rockhopper penguin ('*Eudyptes chrysocomus*')
and little penguin ('*Eudyptula minor*').
Walter Lawry Buller,
A History of the Birds of New Zealand,
London, 1872–3

Buller was a bona fide native of New Zealand, born at the
northern tip of the North Island to a Cornish missionary.
Apparently struggling to fund his research, he sold his
collection of skins to the Colonial Museum, only to find
himself dogged by 'unpalatable and distasteful' claims
by his enemies that he was a mere dealer.

Puffin ('*Fratacula artica*').
Plate by Archibald Thorburn
in Thomas Littleton Powys Lilford, (Baron),
Coloured Figures of the Birds of the British Islands,
London, 1885–97

Archibald Thorburn, a celebrated painter of birds, was
closely associated with the Plumage League, later the
Royal Society for the Protection of Birds. Campaigning
against the killing of birds to decorate hats and
clothing, Thorburn and his buyers were exponents of
the notion that pictures could substitute humanely for
real specimens, rather than acting as a souvenir of a
successful shot.

ABOVE LEFT
Common sexton beetle
('*Silpha vespillo*').

ABOVE RIGHT
Ruby-tailed wasp
('*Chrysis ignita*').

LEFT
Dragonfly; the largest species
('*Libellula grandis*').
All from Edward Donovan,
*The Natural History of British Insects;
Explaining Them in their Several
States, with the Periods of their
Transformations, Etc*.
London, 1793–1813

Shortly after Donovan had concluded
his sixteen-volume series on British
insects, the entomologist William Kirby
complained that little attention was still
paid to insects in his native land: that
entomology was routinely ridiculed as
'trifling ... futile and childish'. One can
only imagine what Donovan made of
this assessment.

TO THE MOST NOBLE
Mary Dutchess of Ormond
this plate is humbly dedicated by Eleazar Albin.

E. Albin del.

H. Fletcher Sculp. London, 1713.

BELOW
'The Lackey'.
Frontispiece, Moses Harris,
The Aurelian,
London, 1766

Harris applied to join the Society of Aurelians at the age of twelve, but was turned down for want of 'sufficient Sagacity'. The strange caption to this picture may indicate Harris' servitude to the Lepidopteran tribe, or it may be a double pun concerning both this and the lackey-moth, named for its stripy caterpillar that apparently resembled a footman's uniform. If the latter, the connection is unfortuitous, the species being 'one of the most injurious species of insects', and highly destructive of fruit trees in its larval form.

OPPOSITE
Painted lady butterfly.
Moses Harris,
The Aurelian,
London, 1766

Harris noticed that this species of butterfly was the most successful in the cold, wet summers of the late 1810s, in which most other species fared very poorly.

The Works of the Lord are Great, Sought out of all them that have Pleasure therein, Ps CXI. v. 2.

To the R.t Hon.ble Lady Charlott
This Plate is most humbly Dedicated

Townshend Baroness Ferrers
by her Ladyships, most obliged & faithful Serv.ts
Moses Harris J.Gretton

PLATE 3.

Lizars sc.

Larvae and chrysalis.
James Duncan,
British Butterflies, Entomology
Vol. 3 in The Naturalist's Library,
Edinburgh, 1835

Appearing in William Jardine and
William Lizars' ambitious series
'The Naturalist's Library', this
volume on butterflies was the
first to append English names to
its pictures, rather than burying
them in the text. The exception
is this plate of caterpillars, which
is simply captioned 'Caterpillars
& Etc.'. It shows the larvae of the
swallowtail (1), pale clouded yellow
(2), hawthorn (3), silver-washed
fritillary (5), purple emperor
(6), white admiral (7), and black
hairstreak (8) butterflies, and the
chrysalis of the black-veined
white (4).

Title page to
Johannes Jonstonus,
Historiae naturalis de insectis,
Frankfurt am Main, 1650–3.
Illustrations by Matthäus
Merian

The engraver and publisher
Matthäus Merian the elder
was the father of Maria Sybilla
Merian, although he died when
she was very young. He was
apparently less committed to
life-drawing than his daughter,
producing visual descriptions
of no fewer than eight
separate species of unicorn.

OVERLEAF
Butterflies.
'*Ordo 3 Insecta Lepidoptera
Genus 1. Papiliones.
Butterflies. Genus 2. Spinges.
Genus 3 Phalenae Moths*'.
James Barbut, *Les genres des
insectes de Linné; constatés
par divers échantillons
d'insectes d'Angleterre,
copiés d'après nature*
('The genera insectorum
of Linnaeus exemplified in
various specimens of English
insects drawn from nature').
Text in English and French.
London, 1781

This spread of butterflies
replicates the layout of a
collector's drawer. The visually
anomalous species numbered
9, not displayed with its wings
pinned out, is the death's-head
hawk moth (the largest native
British moth).

HISTORIÆ NATVRA-
lis de Insectis. Libri. III.
de Serpentibus et Draconib, Libri II
Cum æneis Figuris
IOHANNES IONSTO
nus Med. Doctor
Concinnavit
FRANCOFURTI
ad Mœnum
Impensis
Hæredum Merianorū
MDC LIII.

M. Merian Iun. Inuentor

Genus 3 Phalenæ. Moths.

Ja. Barbut del.

London, Publish'd

1. _Papiliones. Butterflies._

Genus 2. _Sphinges._

'Gryllus Migratorius. Migratory Locust'.
Edward Donovan,
The Natural History of British Insects ...,
London, 1793–1813

In 1748 several small flocks of the migratory locust (of biblical plague fame) were seen near London, where they 'caused much consternation', according to authors of that time. No specimens were preserved. Donovan was obliged to Lady Aylesford who, in September 1799, found this one in a barley field in Warwickshire. It lived several days after its arrival in London, and he thought it would probably have survived much longer had it not been injured in the journey, and weakened by its long confinement.

Insects.
Jakob Hoefnagel,
Diversae insectarum volatilium icons ad vivum accuratissime depictae per ... J.H. ...,
Amsterdam, 1630

This composite image shows both lifelike, shadowed specimens that align Hoefnagel with Dürer and the new true-to-life tradition, and flattened examples more reminiscent of medieval illustration. Hoefnagel was the first artist to concentrate his efforts on insects and to make them the focus of his work, describing the volume as 'a pattern or copy-book for artists [that] displayed on sixteen plates about 340 insects, mostly larger than life'. These may be the earliest printed figures of magnified objects.

OPPOSITE
Spiders.
Eleazer Albin,
Aranei or a Natural History of Spiders,
London, 1793

'With great pains and labour' Albin
managed to collect almost 200 species
of spider for his book. At additional
cost, the reader could obtain a copy
which showed each kind 'beautified in
its proper colours'.

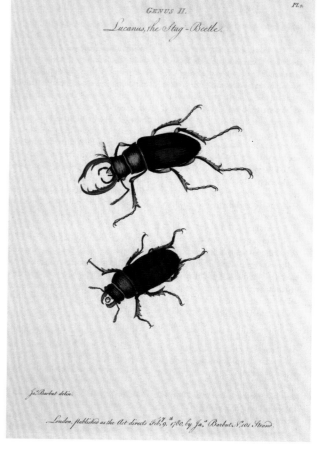

LEFT
Beetles.
Edward Donovan,
The Natural History of British Insects …,
London, 1793–1813

RIGHT
Stag beetle.
James Barbut,
*Les genres des insectes de Linné, constatés par
divers échantillons d'insectes d'Angleterre, copiés
d'après nature* ('The genera insectorum of
Linnaeus exemplified in various specimens of
English insects drawn from nature'). Text in
English and French. London, 1781

There are over 4,000 species of beetle in Britain;
of these, the stag beetle is the most magnificent.

Small horseshoe bat.
Edward Donovan,
*The Natural History
of British Quadrupeds*,
London, 1820

London Pub.d as the Act directs by E.Donovan & F.C.J.Rivingtons. July 1.1814.

'*The Long-eared Bat*'.
William MacGillivray,
*A History of British
Quadrupeds*,
London, 1843.
A volume in Jardine's The
Naturalist's Library

Rumours of vampire bats had
circulated in Europe since the
days of the conquistadors. By
the late eighteenth century
they had become conflated
with other gothic motifs;
the fact that bats like to
roost in old buildings such
as tumbledown castles and
churches (hence are seen
flitting above graveyards)
contributed to their spooky
allure. The bats on both these
pages, though appearing in
natural-historical publications,
are portrayed within this
tradition.

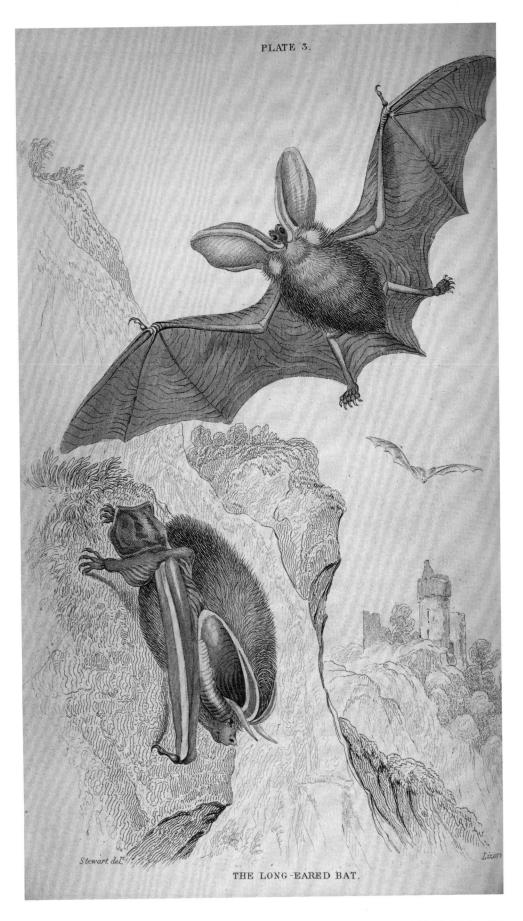

PLATE 3.

Stewart del.

Lizars

THE LONG-EARED BAT.

Auguſt. Joh. Roeſel Inv. et pinx.   M. Tyroff Sculp.

Frontispiece,
August Johann Roesel
von Rosenhof,
*Historia naturalis ranarum
nostratium*,
Nuremberg, 1758

The Latin motto from Virgil
translates as: 'the greatest
wonder may be derived from
observation of the slightest
things', a sentiment that was
routinely and piously echoed
by natural historians.

Frogs.
August Johann Roesel
von Rosenhof,
*Historia naturalis ranarum
nostratium*,
Nuremberg, 1758

Frogs are most familiar creatures,
thriving in the still waters created by
mill-ponds. Collected here, they were
investigated by natural historians
and natural philosophers. Being
vertebrates that metamorphosed
like insects, frogs formed an
important link in the great chain of
nature between the lower animals
(invertebrates) and the higher ones
(typically mammals and birds).

Frogs.
George Edwards, E. Kirkius, et al.,
'Amphibians and reptiles',
(a manuscript collection of original
drawings and watercolours),
first half of eighteenth century

These illustrations are distressing,
because they seem to show actual
frogs, not in natural poses but ready
for dissection or even vivisection.
Frogs were early subjects for
experimentation into respiration
and nervous conduction.

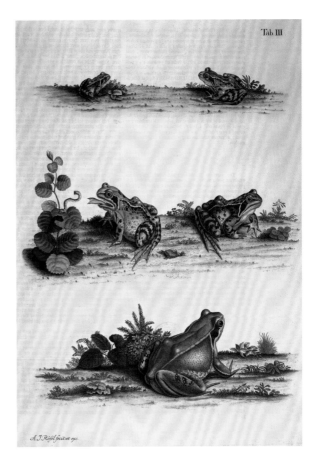

Dessiné par M. WOLF.　　　　　　　　　　　　　　　　　　　Publié chez A. ARNZ et Comp.ᵉ à LEIDE.

LE GROËNLANDAIS, FAUCON BLANC MUÉ.

Domestic

The biological and cultural history of *Homo sapiens* is knitted together with that of many other animal species. Dogs, goats, bees, and fish are among many beasts to have been trained, bred, eaten, and farmed by humankind. The Roman natural historian Pliny the Elder was greatly interested in domesticated animals in his *Naturalis historia* ('Natural History'), and from a twenty-first-century perspective some of his examples seem far from obvious. The *Murex* snail was one such, highly prized as a source of the purple dye used for royal robes. Fish farming and oyster farming are discussed in detail by Pliny; he notes the apparently common problem of owners who become too fond of their fish.

Yet despite the entangled relationships between *Homo sapiens* and other species of animal, the pictorial recording of the species that live alongside humans has lagged behind that of other creatures. Domestic animals, perhaps even more than native species, often remained beneath the radar of scientific and aesthetic interest, until their nature was highlighted by encounters with more exotic kinds, or through the application of new modes of seeing.

In seventeenth-century Italy the Lincei used their new-fangled microscopes to look at bees, and in so doing found fresh interest in these hitherto familiar creatures, now revealed as 'lion-maned, multi-tongued, hairy-eyed'. Pliny, too, had discussed beekeeping, and these domestic animals have for centuries provided a popular model for human lives, domesticated in the city or the polity. Ruled over by the king (as it was thought), bees conducted their lives with busy-ness and good organisation, producing a sweet and useful harvest for the common good. Moderns as much as early moderns found much to admire and emulate in these ancient and wonderful domestic animals. However, bees did not sit easily in the aesthetic conventions spawned by 'from the life' injunctions; to be visible on the page they had to be amplified – artificially magnified. They were not, intuitively or pragmatically, creatures of the same sort as birds, mammals, or reptiles.

Creatures historically associated with the aristocracy are the exception to the generalisation that domestic animals have been little recorded in visual form. The aristocratic pastimes of falconry and hunting have long enjoyed artistic celebration, with treasured birds and dogs often featured in human portraiture. Books and pictures of hunting birds have been particularly beautiful and expensive, complementing the value of well-bred and trained falcons. The *Traité de fauconnerie* (1844–53) is one of the most beautiful animal books ever produced.

During the Agricultural Revolution, a sense arose that improved animal husbandry deserved commemoration for the nation, and for science. Cows and horses

Greenland falcon.
Hermann Schlegel and
Abraham Henrik Verster de Wulverhorst,
Traité de fauconnerie,
Leiden, 1844–53

Widely regarded as the most beautiful book on falconry ever produced, and now extremely rare, the *Traité de Fauconnerie* highlights the difficulty that often occurs in correctly attributing artistic credit for animal images. Line-drawing, engraving, and lithography or hand-painting were all separate processes, highly skilled in themselves. Yet the author is given the highest prominence, and sometimes the artists were not mentioned at all. This book tells us that its seventeen plates were drawn and engraved by Sunderland, Wulf, Allais, 'and other artists'. Wulf's first initial is given wrongly – a sign, perhaps, of the lack of public recognition that artists suffered.

'*The Merino Sheep*'.
Engraving by F. Specht
for No. 9 in Cassell's Natural
History Wall Sheets,
late nineteenth century

Joseph Banks attempted to
improve the British supply of
wool by importing merinos to
Kew Gardens (then George
III's own farm) in 1802.
Domestication in Australia was
far more successful, though
not without major impact upon
native flora, fauna and persons.

were painted by society portraitists, and anatomists honed their representational skills on domestic animal corpses as well as humans. Thomas Bewick's *A General History of Quadrupeds* (1790), originally aimed at children, performed a work of domestication upon many creatures, as well as presenting those of distant origin. His series of pictures began with familiar breeds of horse, cow, mule, pig, and so on, before proceeding to more exotic varieties of like-kind. Eventually the book passed to stranger beasts – to cameleopard, tapir, and hippopotamus – but maintained the domestic frame, introducing the lion, for example, as an 'Animal of the cat-kind'.

Just as it had done for native creatures, so the nineteenth century democratised natural-historical pursuits concerning domestic creatures. Pigeon-fancying was an ancient pursuit and in nineteenth-century London there were a number of breeders' clubs; Charles Darwin belonged to two of them. Thus pigeon-breeding formed an easily recognised entrée to Darwin's argument in *On the Origin of Species* (1859). Though the twenty or so popular varieties of pigeon in existence were all very different, breeders knew that – against all visual odds – they were produced one from another. This selective breeding formed the model for understanding the same process as it was conducted by nature – that is, natural selection – upon the animal varieties existing upon the Earth. Thanks to Darwin's work, breaking down the scientific boundaries between varieties and species, domestic animals too were now a part of natural history.

Specht

A. Specht lith.

M. Seeger imp.

THE MERINO SHEEP.

Bees and beehive.
Original watercolour (manuscript dedicated to Elizabeth I), sixteenth century

This watercolour formed the basis for the engraved title page of Thomas Moffett's *Insectorum sive minimorum animalium theatrum* (1634). Bees came to prominence as the poster-insect for human society in the eighteenth century. The image of their hard work, building up the economic stock of the commonweal, was almost irresistible. Adam Smith dismissed Bernard Mandeville's 1714 book, *The Fable of the Bees*, subtitled 'private vices, publick benefits', as 'wholly pernicious'. Much depended upon the bees' moral motivations: were they working for the good of all, or only doing so because that was the best way to serve themselves?

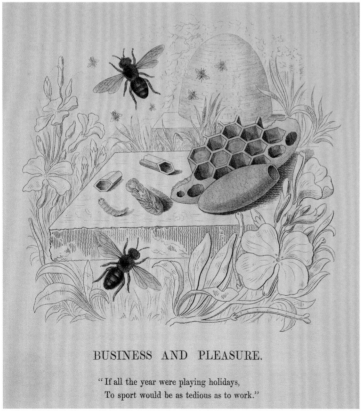

BUSINESS AND PLEASURE.

"If all the year were playing holidays,
To sport would be as tedious as to work."

Bees and honeycomb
('*Business and Pleasure.
"If all the years were playing holidays, To sport would be as tedious as to work"'*).
Louisa M. Budgen
(pseudonym: 'Acheta Domestica'),
Episodes of Insect Life,
London, 1867

By the nineteenth century, bee-inspired questions of political economy had generally deteriorated into personal moral blandishments.

Bees.
('*Queen, Worker, Drone*').
Samuel Bagster,
The Management of Bees,
London, 1834

By the very end of the
nineteenth century,
suspicion had fallen upon
the male drones (bottom),
raised at great cost by
the nest but of little value
beyond their brief role in
fertilisation. *Fin-de-siècle*
commentators hastened
to compare them to social
parasites in humanity –
their exact identification
depending upon the
prejudices of the writers
(antisemitic, prohibitionist,
to name but two).

Historian Ben Marsh describes
the idyllic picture painted of
sericulture in descriptions of life
in the new American colonies.
One poetic account ran:

> *Here tend the Silkworm
> in the verdant Shade
> The frugal Matron,
> and the blooming Maid.
> Th'expiring Insect's
> curious Work resume,
> And wind Materials for
> the British Loom.*

London fancy canaries
('*Jonque Cock, Mealy Hen, Mealy Nesting*').
W. A. Blakston,
*The Illustrated Book of Canaries and
Cage-Birds, British and Foreign,*
London 1877–80

Scholars have discovered an Italian painting
from the 1490s showing completely yellow birds
that may be canaries, suggesting that selective
breeding of these popular domestic birds may
have occurred in Italy before this date. Conrad
Gessner, in 1555, described a specific type of
partially yellow canary from Italy, and stated that
these specially bred birds were transported to
Germany, which is where selective breeding is
known to have occurred.

RIGHT
'Ring Pigeon'.
Title page,
Prideaux John Selby,
Ornithology, Vol. 5,
Jardine's The Naturalist's Library,
Edinburgh, 1835

The astonishing variety of domestic pigeons provided Darwin with his killer analogy (artificial/natural selection) in *On the Origin of Species* (1859). Darwin joined two of the London pigeon clubs, and kept every breed that he could lay his hands upon. The pouter, he noted, 'has a much elongated body, wings, and legs; and its enormously developed crop, which it glories in inflating, may well excite astonishment and even laughter'.

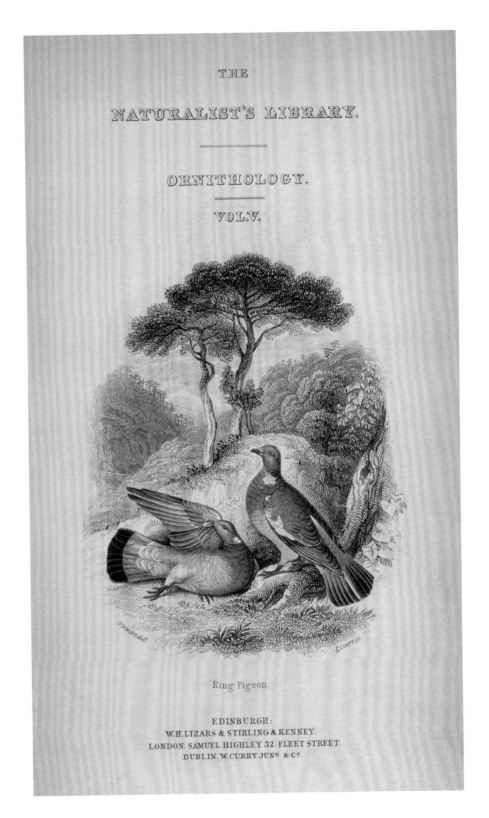

THE

NATURALIST'S LIBRARY.

ORNITHOLOGY.

VOL. V.

Ring Pigeon.

EDINBURGH:
W.H. LIZARS & STIRLING & KENNEY.
LONDON. SAMUEL HIGHLEY 32. FLEET STREET.
DUBLIN. W. CURRY JUNᴿ & Cᵒ.

Title page, George Turberville,
The Booke of Faulconrie or Hauking for the Onely Delight and pleasure of all Noblemen and Gentlemen,
London, 1575

A princely lady found in some of this book's illustrations is apparently Queen Elizabeth herself. Hawking was practised by gentlewomen from medieval times until the nineteenth century, at which point it became restricted to masculine circles.

OPPOSITE
Frontispiece, Hermann Schlegel and Abraham Henrik Verster de Wulverhorst,
Traité de fauconnerie,
Leiden, 1844–53

The frontispiece to the *Traité* shows the birds not only in the field, but also at the card table and even in church.

The Booke of Faulconrie or Hau-
KING, FOR THE ONELY DE-
light and pleasure of all Noblemen and Gentlemen:
Collected out of the best aucthors, asvvell Italians as Frenchmen,
and some English practises withall concernyng Faulconrie, the contentes
whereof are to be seene in the next page folowyng.
By *George Turberuile* Gentleman.
NOCET EMPTA DOLORE VOLVPTAS.

Imprinted at London for Christopher Barker, at the signe of
the Grashopper in Paules Churchyarde. *Anno.* 1575.

Mon espoir est en pennes.

TRAITÉ
DE
FAUCONNERIE
par
H. Schlegel
et
A.H. Verster de Wulverhorst.

Leiden et Düsseldorf
chez
Arnz & Comp
1844 – 1853.

Erfunden u. auf Stein gez. von J.B. Sonderland.

PHEASANT.

'*Pheasant Shooting*'.
Henry Thomas Alken,
The National Sports of Great Britain,
London, 1903

Common pheasants have been found amongst Roman remains in Britain, although it is questioned whether these were bred in the country. Saxon references to the birds are disputed; it is believed that these may refer to the capercaillie instead. The widespread introduction of the pheasant, originating in Asia, occurred within a century or so of the Norman Conquest (1066). Since then they have become a mainstay of the British countryside, and a favourite bird for hunting. Questions about the pheasant's presence in the archaeological record are compounded by the fact that its bones are difficult to distinguish from those of other fowl, especially after destruction through the process of preparation for the table.

H. Alken delt.   London, Published by T. McLean, Jan.y 1, 1820.   J. Clark sculpt.

PHEASANT SHOOTING.

THE TERRIER.

Sydenham Edwards was primarily a
botanical illustrator and one gets the
distinct feeling that his book of dogs
was a very personal labour of love. His
account wove dogs deep into the historic
fabric of the nation. 'England has long
been eminent for the superiority of her
dogs', he noted – although as historian
Harriet Ritvo has shown, dog breeds in
the modern sense only emerged in the
century after Edwards' book appeared.

THE POINTER

A. Specht lith.

M. Seeger imp.

THE NEWFOUNDLAND DOG.

'*The Newfoundland Dog*'.
Engraving by F. Specht for No. 6 in
Cassell's Natural History Wall Sheets,
late nineteenth century

The Victorian circus performer known as
the 'Thousand Guinea Dog Napoleon' was
supposedly a Newfoundland. Beginning
his career ridden by human jockeys, he
apparently progressed to being able to
spell out 'God Save the Queen'.

Cat.
Conrad Gessner,
Historiae animalium,
Tiguri, 1551–8

Mary, Queen of Scots,
embroidered a cat based
upon this picture.

Domestic cats ('*Felis domestica*').
Daniel Geraud Elliot,
*A Monograph of the Felidae,
or Family of the Cats*,
New York, 1878

Cats have, with certain exceptions,
progressed from witches' familiars to
charming domestic companions. This
picture is definitely at the latter end of
the representational scale.

FELIS DOMESTICA

'*The Dutch Rabbit*'.
Leonard U. Gill,
*The Book of the Rabbit,
Giving the History, Variations,
Uses, Points ... of Fancy Rabbits*,
London, 1881

Recent genetic science suggests
a single origin for the domestic
rabbit, from wild populations in
France, within the past 1,500 years.
This accords with historical records
that place rabbit domestication in
French monasteries. Rabbits are now
quite popular as pets, and as this
book indicates, varieties have been
developed for show; but the vast
majority of rabbit-keeping has been
for food, not companionship.

Turkey ('*Gallopavo Christatus. The Crested Turkey Cock*'). Eleazar Albin, *A Natural History of Birds*, London, 1738

The turkey was domesticated in Central America – most likely by the Mayans – at least 2,000 years ago. How it came to be named for the land of Istanbul is a matter of some historical debate, but reflects the general etymological orientalism of the British. In Turkey it is known as a 'Hindi' – presumably 'Indian' in the same sense that Native Americans were.

Domestic muscovy drake, and frog. From a miscellaneous collection of natural history drawings by Indian artists working in Murshidabad and Calcutta, *c.* 1806–10

These two creatures, though zoologically quite distinct, are both a familiar sight at the domestic pond.

RIGHT
'Dorking Hen'.
Martin Doyle,
*The Illustrated Book
of Domestic Poultry*,
London, 1854

BELOW
Chicken.
Ulisse Aldrovandi,
Ornithologiae, Bologna, 1646

The domestic chicken has an ancient and culturally diverse natural history in conjunction with humankind. Aldrovandi devoted a tenth of his ornithology to chickens. Besides their value in supplying meat and eggs, he noted their value in medicine: 'precisely what body's illness ... does not obtain its remedies hence?' Chicken soup for the soul and body, indeed.

DORKING HEN.

Plate XVI.

THE OLD LINCOLN BREED.
Ram, bred by Mr Jex, St Jennings, near Lynne, County of Norfolk.
PROFESSOR LOW'S ILLUSTRATIONS OF THE BREEDS OF THE DOMESTIC ANIMALS
Published June, 1841, by Longman, Orme, Brown, Green & Longmans, Paternoster Row, London

Sheep ('*The Old Lincoln Breed*').
David Low,
*The Breeds of the Domestic Animals
of the British Islands*,
London, 1842

The Old Lincoln was a variety of sheep bred for
the lowland field rather than for the hillside. As
such it was larger and had longer and thicker
wool, suitable for the hard, smooth worsteds that
went into woollen suits. David Low held British
wool, such as the Lincoln's, to be unbeatable
for these purposes.

*'1. The four horned Ram,
2. Horns of the Iceland Sheep,
3. Horns of the Cretan Sheep'.*
Ebenezer Sibly,
*An Universal System of Natural
History Including the Natural
History of Man, etc.,*
London, 1794–1807

An astrologer, freemason, and
mesmerist, Sibly was not the usual
sort of naturalist for his period. He
believed that recent discoveries in
science could refresh magical and
hermetic traditions. These cloven-
footed creatures seem to promise
mysteries of some sort, even
though, here, the accompanying
text is quite unremarkable and
factual in nature.

The four horned Ram. 2. Horns of the Iceland Sheep.
3. Horns of the Cretan Sheep.

Alpaca ('*The Alpacos, Zoological Gardens*').
Characteristic Sketches of Animals,
principally in the Zoological Gardens,
Regent's Park, drawn from the life and
engraved by Thomas Landseer: with
descriptive ... notices by J. H. Barrow,
London, 1832

Thomas Landseer was best known for his
engravings and etchings. He apparently drew this
specimen at the gardens of the Zoological Society
of London, founded three years earlier and not yet
open to the public. Landseer's older brother, the
painter Edwin Landseer, had taken up residence
near the gardens, in Regent's Park, a couple of
years previously.

THE ALPACOS.

ZOOLOGICAL GARDENS.

London. Published Jan.7 1.1831. by Moon, Boys & Graves. Printsellers to the King. 3. Pall Mall.

ABOVE
Alpaca.
Henrick Brouwer,
*A Voyage to the Kingdom
of Chili in America*,
London, 1732

BELOW
Alpaca.
Philip Lutley Sclater,
*Zoological Sketches by Joseph Wolf
Made for the Zoological Society of
London, from Animals in their Vivarium
in the Regent's Park*,
London, 1861

Recent scientific research dates domestication of the alpaca to an almost incredible 6,000–7,000 years before the present day in the Peruvian Andes. DNA evidence strongly suggests that – hybridisation notwithstanding – it is a descendant of the vicuña, and not the guanaco, as previously thought. As a result of this, its modern species name has been amended.

Drawn by Mr Nicholson, R.S.A. from a Painting by Mr Shiels, R.S.A.

Drawn on Stone & Printed by Fairland.

Pig ('*Old English Breed, Drawn by Mr. Nicholson from a Painting by Mr Shiels, RSA*'), David Low, *The Breeds of the Domestic Animals of the British Islands*, London, 1842

Low was moved to contemplate the relatively dramatic and yet speedy domestication of the pig in comparison to other species. 'Anecdotes of the habits, the courage, and strength, of this wild and solitary creature are interesting as facts of natural history, and likewise physiologically, as shewing the vast change which domestication produces on his characters: and not more remarkable is the ... readiness with which he yields up his natural instinct and resigns himself to bondage.'

'A Beautiful Yorkshire Cow. Bred & Fatted by A. F. Foljambe Esq.
at Osberton Notts. by a Bull of Mr Coate's the sire of the Dritfield
Cow the Dam of Patriot which was sold for 500 Guineas'.
George Garrard,
*A Description of the Different Varieties
of Oxen Common in the British Isles,*
London, 1800

It is notoriously difficult to convert prices from one period to
another, as relative values change. However, 500 guineas, the
cost of the animal in question, is somewhere in the range of
a high-end luxury car today.
    The caption also helpfully gives the following vital statistics:
'Height of Shoulder 4ft 10in, From Pole to Tail 7ft 2in,
Round Chest 8ft, Shin Bone 8in. Live Weight 168 stone 9lb,
4 quarters 98 stone 11lb, Fat 11 stone 1lb. 12 Years Old'.

Zebu bull ('*Bos indicus*').
Watercolour by unknown Indian artist,
c. 1798–1805, from Marquess Wellesley
Collection of Natural History Drawings

Now classified *Bos taurus indicus*, the zebu
originated in south-east Asia but had been
exported to Egypt as early as 2000 BCE. It is
very resistant to heat but gives less milk, and
poorer quality meat, than European cattle.

OVERLEAF
'The Chillingham Bull'.
Woodcut by Thomas Bewick executed for
Marmaduke Tunstall of Wycliffe

The Agricultural Revolution produced many
remarkable specimens of animal life. At a time when
natural-historical pictures were usually generalised
representations drawn from several specimens,
books like this commemorated particular
individuals – celebrity animals. Here we see
'The Ox of Houghton le Spring', which hailed
from near Durham, was grass-fed, and
weighed in at 200 stone (1,270 kg).

'*The Old English Black Horse. Stallion by Old Blacklegs by a Mare of the Dishley breed – bred by Mr. Broomes at Ormiston, Derby*'.
David Low,
The Breeds of the Domestic Animals of the British Islands,
London, 1842

Low reckoned this race of horses to be indigenous across Europe and the Near East. It was used by the Romans, and then by their barbarian attackers, at which time 'the Great Black Horse of the North became an instrument of destruction, and an object of terror'.

THE OLD ENGLISH BLACK HORSE.
Stallion, by old Blacklegs, from a Mare of the Dishley breed .— bred by Mr Broomes, at Ormiston, Derby.
PROFESSOR LOW'S ILLUSTRATIONS OF THE BREEDS OF THE DOMESTIC ANIMALS.

'The Clydesdale Breed. Stallion, 7 years old, the property of Mr. Low, Morton, near Edinburgh, with a Zetland Bay, the property of the Rt. Hon. the Earl of Hopetoun'.
David Low,
The Breeds of the Domestic Animals of the British Islands,
London, 1842

The Clydesdale, a draught horse, made up in useful qualities what it lacked in racial purity. Such seems to be Low's take on the creature. Questions about bloodline and inheritance in domestic animals were trial runs for similar debates concerning human evolution.

THE CLYDESDALE BREED.
Stallion, 7 Years old, the property of Mr Low, Morton, near Edinburgh, with a Zetland Bay the property of the Rt Hon.ble the Earl of Hopetoun.
PROFESSOR LOW'S ILLUSTRATIONS OF THE BREEDS OF THE DOMESTIC ANIMALS.

OVERLEAF
'Geometrical Drawing representing the exact proportions of the late Famous Eclipse'.
Charles Vial de Saint Bel,
Elements of the Veterinary Art, containing an Essay on the Proportions of the Celebrated Eclipse,
London, 1797

The visual presentation of this undefeated eighteenth-century British Thoroughbred racehorse recalls the Vitruvian Man of Leonardo, perfect in every proportion. The anatomical component that became most valuable after his retirement (he sired around 350 winners) is curiously downplayed, however. Eclipse was bred by the Duke of Cumberland. The entire English Thoroughbred line, including Eclipse, was descended from three Arab stallions imported in the seventeenth and eighteenth centuries.

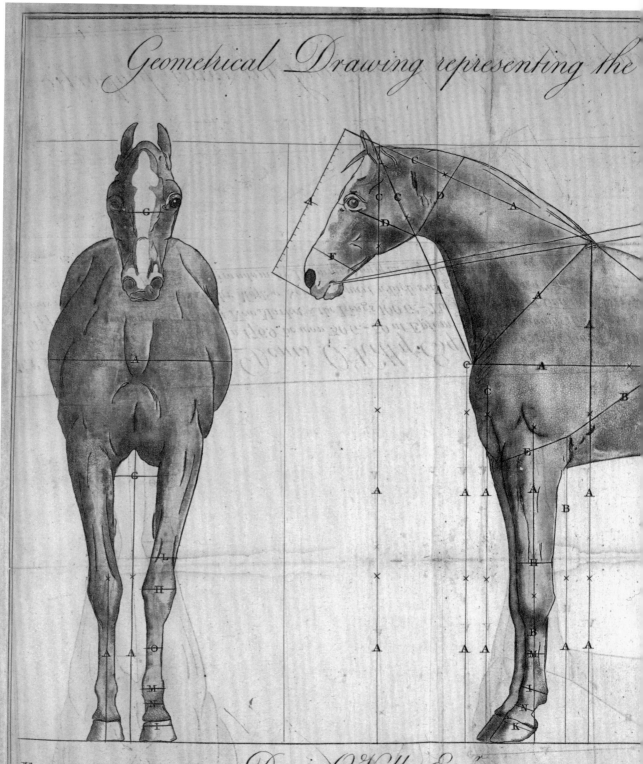

Geometrical Drawing representing the

ECLIPSE was the property of *Denis O'Kelly Esqr* was bred by the late D: of C
to his Late - possessor for 1700 Gs. In 1769 he won 50 G. - 50 at Epsom - 50 at Ascotheath Heath - the
In 1779 he receiv'd forfeit 600 Gs. at New Market & the King's 100 Gs. - The King's 100 G. at Guildford - D.
He was never beat. - Eclipse was got by Mask a Son of Squirt which was got by Bartlets Childers his Da
Grandam by Hautboy his Gt. Gt. Gt. Grandam by Brimmer Son of the Oglethorps Arabian he Died the 27th

London. Prin

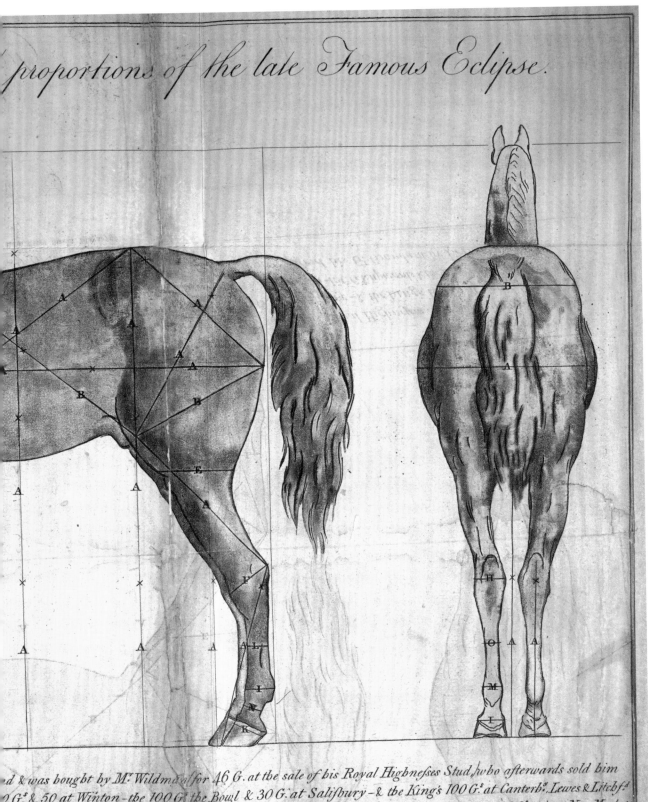

proportions of the late Famous Eclipse.

...d & was bought by M.ʳ Wildman for 46 G. at the sale of his Royal Highneſses Stud, who afterwards sold him

...0 G.ˢ & 50 at Winton – the 100 G.ˢ the Bowl & 30 G. at Saliſbury – & the King's 100 G.ˢ at Canterb.ʸ, Lewes & Litchf.ᵈ

...gham – D.º & 319ᵍ.10ˢ at York – the King's 100 G. at Lincoln – 150 G. & upwards & the King's 100 G.ˢ again at New Market,

...gulus his Grandam by a full brother to Wildmans Squirrel his G.ᵗ Grandam by L.ᵈ Darceys Montagu his G.ᵗ G.ᵗ

...ʳ 1789 in the 26.ᵗʰ Year of his Age.

...rtin & Rain, Fleet Street, May 1.1795.

OPPOSITE
Ornamental goldfish
('*Kin-Yu. Le Superbe*').
Edme Billardon-Sauvigny,
Histoire naturelle des dorades de la Chine
('Natural History of the Goldfish of China'),
Paris, 1780

Different types of carp (family Cyprinidae) have been farmed for eating for thousands of years. The emergence of the genetic mutation that causes the golden coloration of the genus Carassius within this family (the familiar goldfish) is recorded during the Chinese Jin dynasty (265–420 CE). Later mutants successfully established as breeding stock are very specifically noted within historical records.

Cyprinus.   Carpe.   The Carp.   Eleazar Albin delineavit

'The Carp'.
Coloured engraving by Eleazar Albin
from Roger North,
A Treatise on Fish and Fish-ponds,
London, 1825

KIN-YU.

Le Superbe

Dessiné en Chine

Gravé par Martinet

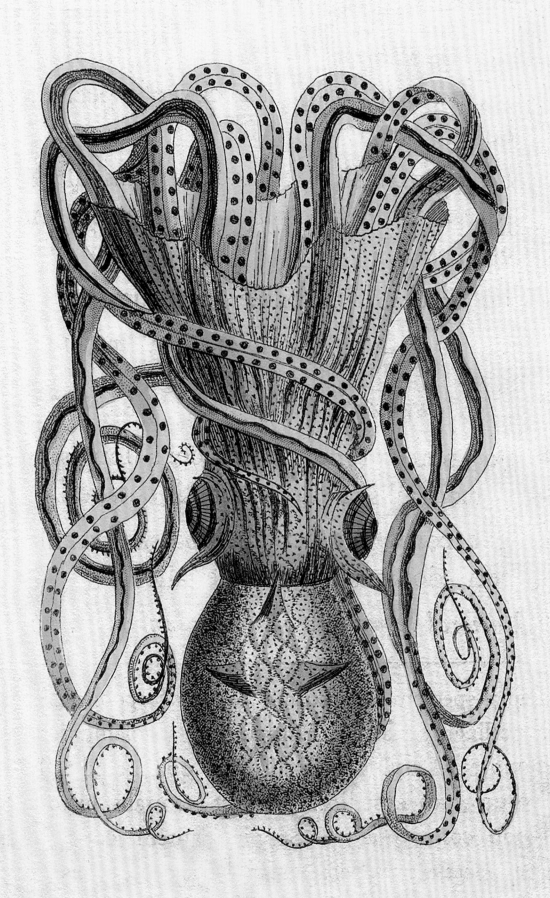

Paradoxical

The ocean is understandably a source of terror, and tales of giant squid or octopuses are one way of making such fears manifest. In 1802, the French naturalist Pierre Denys de Montfort posited the existence of two such species. This example from a British book of the same era is truly the stuff of nightmares, coyly curled onto the page, but threatening to escape.

Since medieval times, writers and illustrators have enjoyed the spectacle of creatures that appear to transgress the human/animal boundary. Such monsters often originated in ancient myth (written up by Pliny) and were lightly Christianised as demonstrating the limitless wealth of God's creation. Ambroise Paré's *Des Monstres et Prodiges* ('On Monsters and Marvels', 1573) famously presented such marvellous curiosities – human births that were partly animal in nature. Altogether in early modern libraries there were hordes of centaurs and satyrs, and a veritable plague of bishop-fish.

It was quite natural for such creatures to appear in early animal books. Thus, for example, Edward Topsell drew the lamia for his *History of Four-footed Beasts* (1607): a monster with both hooved and clawed feet, with human breasts and a female face, and covered in scales. Conrad Gessner's lamia, recorded half a century earlier, is apparently a shark – possibly a great white – a creature which still troubles us today: a monster of the modern imagination.

For a time, perhaps, it seemed as though the existence of such creatures might be vindicated by the reports returning from the New World. Cashing in on the craze for natural-historical collections in the early modern period, canny sailors and inhabitants of far-flung lands stitched together body parts to make saleable, 'real' monsters. The head of a monkey and tail of a fish, for example, made a plausible mermaid.

Linnaeus included the category 'Animalia paradoxa' in his first few editions of the *Systema naturae* ('The System of Nature', 1735), making space for these borderline creatures. It is hard to know exactly why he did so: from a modern point of view it seems a strange inclusion for a list that otherwise was concerned with very real creatures. For one thing, it was simply unthinkable to have a book of beasts without these traditional inhabitants. Moreover, Linnaeus was very much theologically inspired in his work, and in this sense monstrous beasts were necessary things to think with; they framed his thought even if they were not real. Finally, there were also rumours, reports, and drawings that had at least to be considered. There was a hydra, similar to a creature described in the Book of Revelation, apparently preserved in Hamburg; and a South American frog that was well attested as transforming into a fish. Linnaeus' sceptical mention of a weasel's teeth being transplanted into the head of an amphibian suggests that his list may also have functioned as an appeal for readers to weed out fantastical beasts from the ark of knowledge. 'As long as it is not seen either living or dead,' he wrote, 'nor faithfully and perfectly described, it is called in doubt.'

Other borderline animals include creatures out of place, or out of scale; they create challenges of visual representation just as they do of cognition. Pestiferous creatures surge up, unwanted: nests of rats, worms of decomposition, irritating lice. In medieval and early modern times these unwanted creatures of sickness and decay were considered the corrupted facsimiles of the Devil. Unable to perform genuine works of creation, Satan could nevertheless magic up *faux* beasts, just as the Pharaoh's magicians did in the Book of Exodus. Rats, frogs, and insects were his chief productions; animals that otherwise were quite real and normal were also paradoxical. Robert Hooke's gigantic magnified flea, though emphatically natural and not devilish, nevertheless tests our mental ordering of the world, our assumption that the human scale of things automatically brings superiority.

Even after modern schemes of taxonomy were created they were constantly tested by fresh examples from the natural world. The egg-laying duck-billed platypus was a source of great confusion. But less exotic creatures could be troublesome too. Darwin's seven-year detour into the dissection of barnacles was the result of taxonomic paradox: the creatures had recently been reassigned from the Mollusca to the Articulata, and required a great deal of new study. Darwin was perplexed by much that he saw in these strange creatures, not least their transgressive modes of sex and sexuality. In some specimens he discovered quasi-parasitic males coexisting with hermaphroditic hosts of the same species. Writing in *A Monograph on the Cirripedia* (1851), he professed his instinctive disbelief that such 'diverse beings, with scarcely anything in common [could belong] to the same species!'

Darwin's shock at the barnacles' strange domestic and sexual arrangements speaks to the moral authority of nature: the continuing sense, persisting even to this day, that the animal world validates (or occasionally questions) our own species' choices. In post-Darwinian times, men of science and fairground proprietors alike searched for the 'missing link', that ultimate paradoxical beast, poised on the exact moment of transition from animal to human.

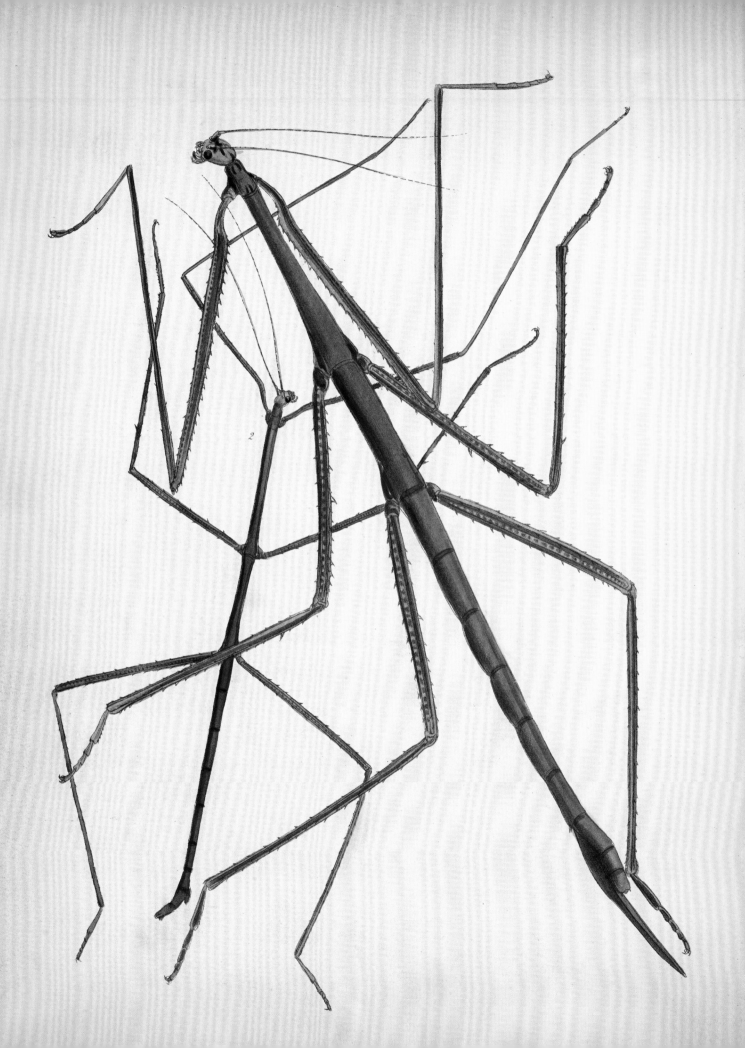

DE MONOCEROTE.

Figura hæc talis est, qualis à pictoribus ferè hodie pingitur, de qua certi nihil habeo.

Unicorn ('*De Monocerote*').
Conrad Gessner,
Historiae animalium,
Tiguri, 1551–8

One of the challenges of natural-historical drawing is the representation of scale. This unicorn may be as small as 71 centimetres (28 inches) in length, the size ascribed to the creatures by the fifth-century BCE writer Ctesias in his book on India. They must have remained this size throughout the Middle Ages, else how could female virgins have caught them on their laps, as all sources agreed that they did?

Manticore.
Edward Topsell,
The History of Four-footed Beasts and Serpents (single-volume edition),
London, 1658

A widely known monster, the manticore is described by Topsell as having 'greatness, roughness, and feet like a lion, face and ears like a man's', and a tail like a scorpion's, often armed with a sting. What is not clearly visible in this picture are its teeth: a triple row on both upper and lower jaws.

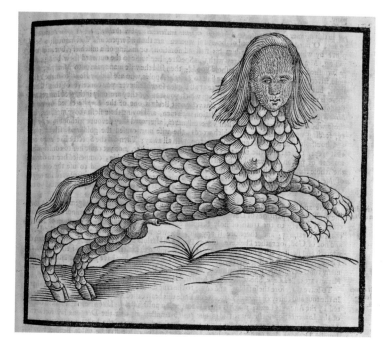

Lamia.
Edward Topsell,
The History of Four-footed Beasts and Serpents (single-volume edition),
London, 1658

No creature in Topsell's volumes stands out as stranger than this lamia. 'When they see a man,' Topsell notes, 'they lay open their breastes, and by the beauty thereof, entice them to come neare to conference, and so ... devoure and kill them.' The picture does not very successfully portray the irresistibility of this alleged temptation.

Five-legged chicken and
two-headed bird.
Ulisse Aldrovandi,
Ornithologiae, Bologna, 1646

Aldrovandi stated that the five-footed rooster
hatched in 125 BCE; among his many other
monstrous specimens were some that he had
seen with his own eyes ...

Chicken ('*Gallus cauda quadrupedis
cum crista Gallinacea*').
Ulisse Aldrovandi,
Ornithologiae, Bologna, 1646

... including this one, which lived in the palace
of the Grand Duke of Tuscany, Francesco I de'
Medici. Aldrovandi recalled that 'it struck fear ...
into brave men with its terrifying aspect'.

'*Flying Fish No. 4*'.
Richard Bridgens,
West India Scenery, London, 1836

Pliny the Elder, in his *Naturalis historia*
('Natural History', 77–79 CE), referred
to a fish known as the sea-swallow,
which, being able to fly, bore a strong
resemblance to the bird of that name.
Early-modern naturalists debated which
species he had in mind.

Flying fish.
Ippolito Salviani,
Aquatilium animalium historiae,
Rome, 1554

The naturalist Guillaume Rondelet noted that these fish flew out of the water in order to avoid being eaten by larger fish. Their flesh, it was agreed, was 'hard and dry', the latter adjective perhaps indicating the absence of characteristics associated with the Aristotelian element of water in this paradoxical, apparently air-breathing variety.

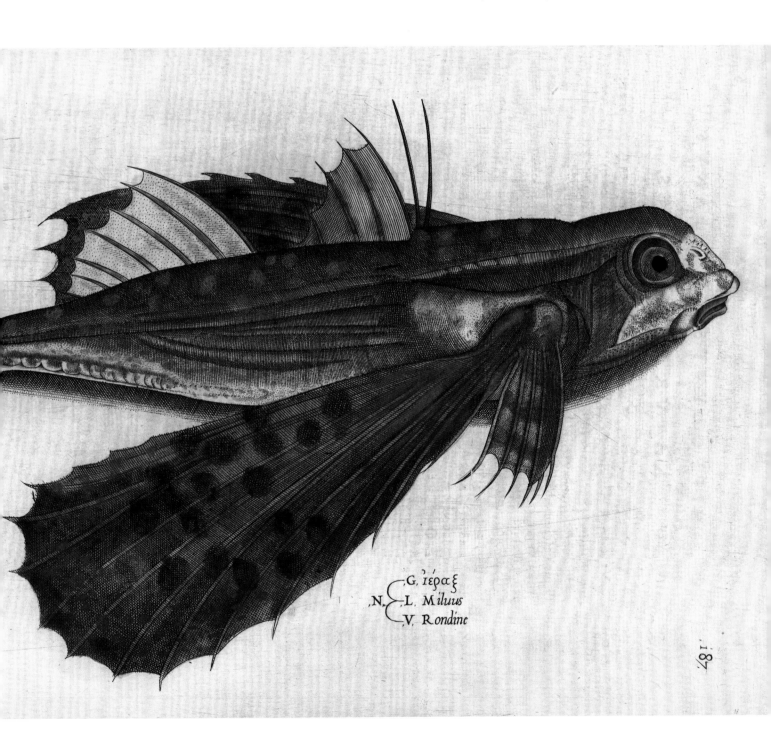

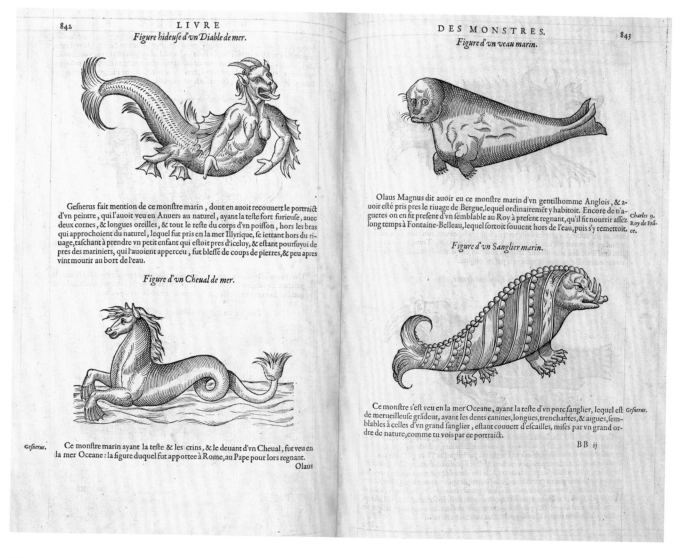

Page of monsters ('*Figure hideuse d'un Diable de mer; Figure d'un Cheval de mer; Figure d'un veau marin; Figure d'un Sanglier marin*').
Ambroise Paré, *Les Oeuvres de M. Ambroise Paré ... Avec les figures & portraicts tant de l'anatomie que des instruments de chirurgie, & de plusiers monstres, etc.*,
Paris, 1575

The sixteenth-century French royal surgeon Ambroise Paré was the author of a definitive book on monsters, strange creatures which brought glory to God. On this page are included a wonderfully literal imagining of a seahorse, and a seal (*veau marin*, 'sea-calf', seen in 1538) that appears quite ordinary until one reads the text: it was 72 feet (22 metres) long, 14 feet high, measured 7 feet between the eyes and had a liver that filled five wine casks.

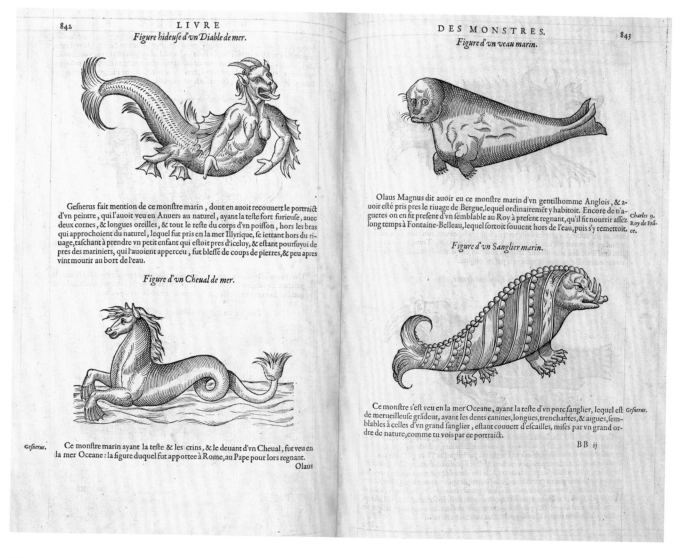

OPPOSITE ABOVE
Mermaid.

OPPOSITE BELOW
Invented creatures(?).
Both from Louis Renard, 'Poissons, écrevisses et crabes ... que l'on trouve autour des Isles Moluques, et sur les côtes des Terres Australes' (manuscript of painted drawings presented to Hans Sloane by Renard), Amsterdam, early eighteenth century

'Poissons, écrevisses et crabes' includes a gamut of specimens from the plausible to the incredible. Thankfully, given Renard's usual gustatory preoccupations, no eating guidance is given for this mermaid, the final specimen in his account. Renard tells us that it was kept captive in a tank for a few days, but would not eat and so died of hunger. After its death, the artist is said to have lifted her fins in the front and back and, in Renard's somewhat voyeuristic phrase, found her to be 'like any other woman'. The fish below look to be somewhere in the middle of Renard's range of believability.

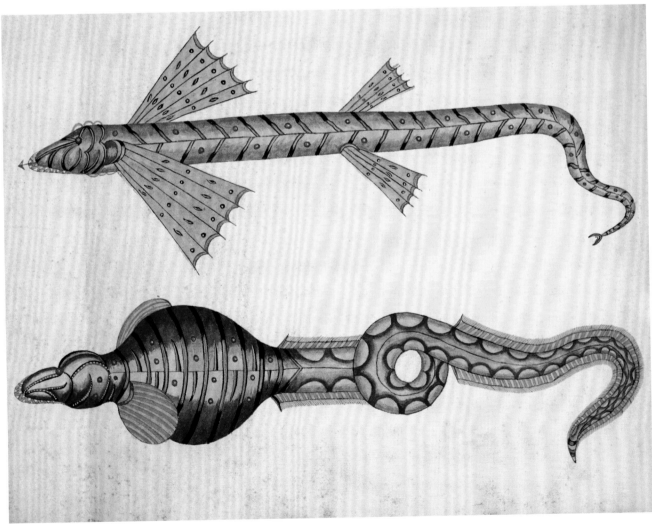

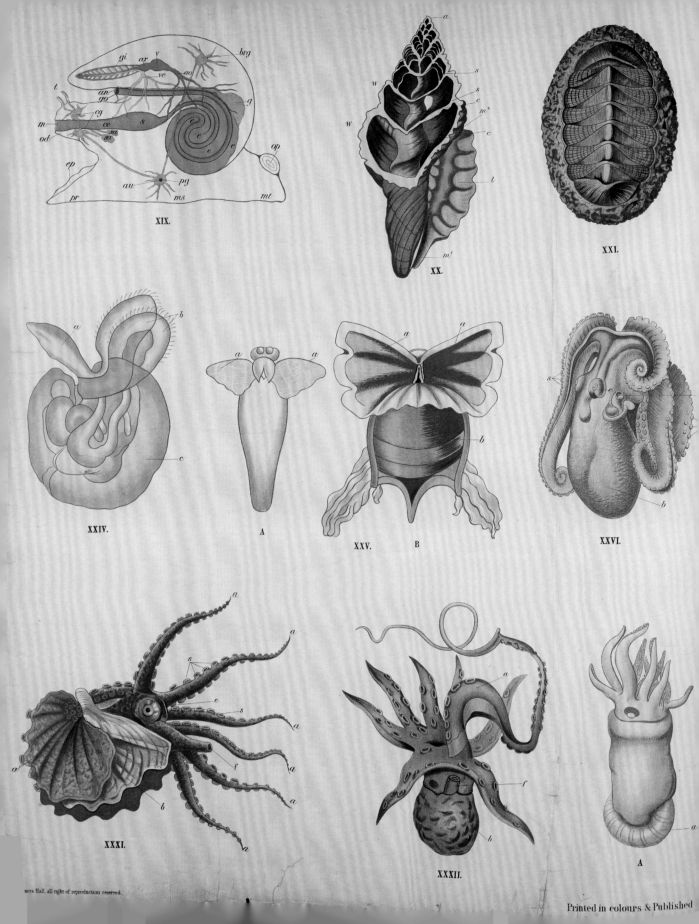

XIX.

XX.

XXI.

XXIV.

A

XXV.

B

XXVI.

XXXI.

XXXII.

A

Printed in colours & Published

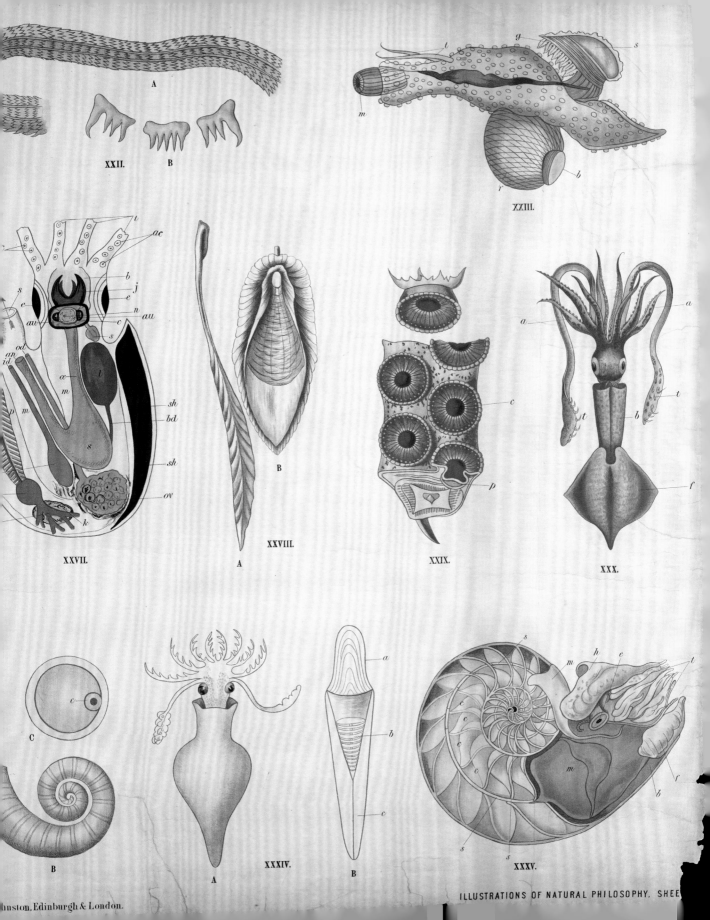

A

XXII.

B

XXIII.

XXVII.

XXVIII.

A

B

XXIX.

XXX.

C

B

XXXIV.

A

B

XXXV.

PREVIOUS PAGES
'Illustrations of Natural Philosophy'.
Printed in colours & published by
W. & A. K. Johnston, Edinburgh and
London. Date unknown, perhaps second
half of the nineteenth century

This spread of images speaks to an emerging distinction
between natural history and zoology around the turn
of the nineteenth century. Zoology is historically more
associated with dissected specimens than it is with *in
situ* observations. It is connected with the discipline of
comparative anatomy, which traced the appearance of
identical organs or bones across various species without
considering their function, as a naturalist might have
been inclined to do.

Anthomedusae. — Blumenquallen.   Tafel 15.

LEFT
Jellyfish
('*Anthomedusae*').
Ernst Haeckel,
Kunstformen der Natur,
Vienna, 1914

G. H. Lewes captured
the paradoxical life cycle
of the medusa, with its
completely different life-
stages, thus: 'Imagine a
lily producing a butterfly,
and the butterfly in turn
producing a lily, and you
would scarcely invent a
marvel greater than this
production of Medusae
was to its first discoverers.'

Starfish ('*Asteridea*').
Ernst Haeckel,
Kunstformen der Natur,
Vienna, 1914

As well as creating as these glorious coloured plates showing 'art forms in nature', Haeckel is known for producing a series of images and models of embryos, rising from fish to human form. Together, these visual representations manifest a grand, romantic, and organic view of the animal kingdom, united in a grand – albeit non-divine – pattern.

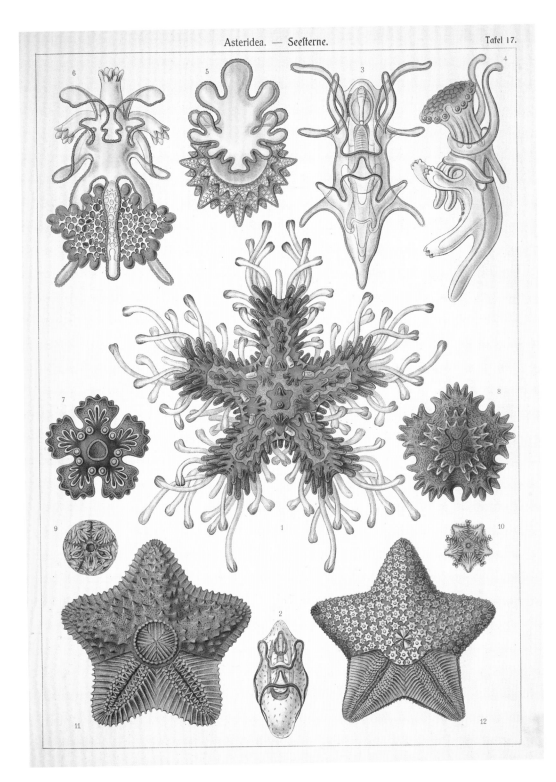

Asteridea. — Seesterne. Tafel 17.

Cuvier established four fundamental types or
embranchements of the animal kingdom. In these
images we see examples of two of them: the
leeches, which are members of the Articulata, and
Mollusca, a group in their own right. The other two
embranchements were Vertebrata (vertebrates) and
Radiata (starfish and jellyfish). Cuvier's insistence that
these four groups were divinely ordained blueprints,
admitting no possibility of intermediary animals,
created an investigatory context in which fresh and
controversial paradoxes were thrown up.

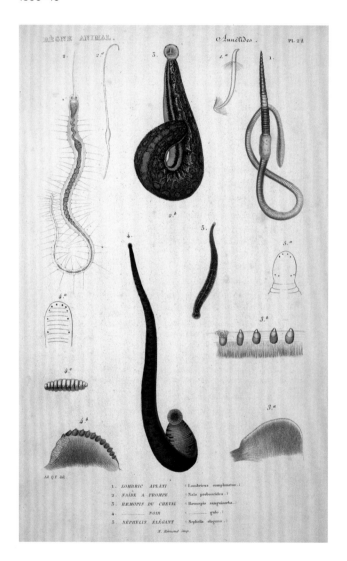

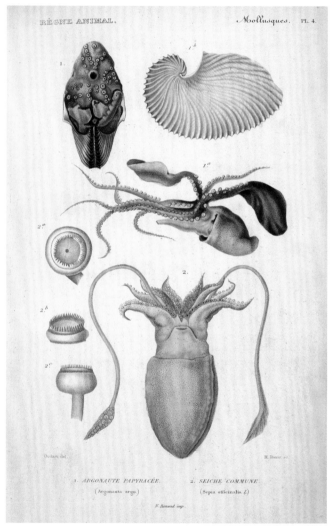

The scorpion transgresses a simplistic but powerful belief
within Western Christian traditions: a creature so far down the
divine hierarchy of size and complexity ought not to be able to
do so much damage.

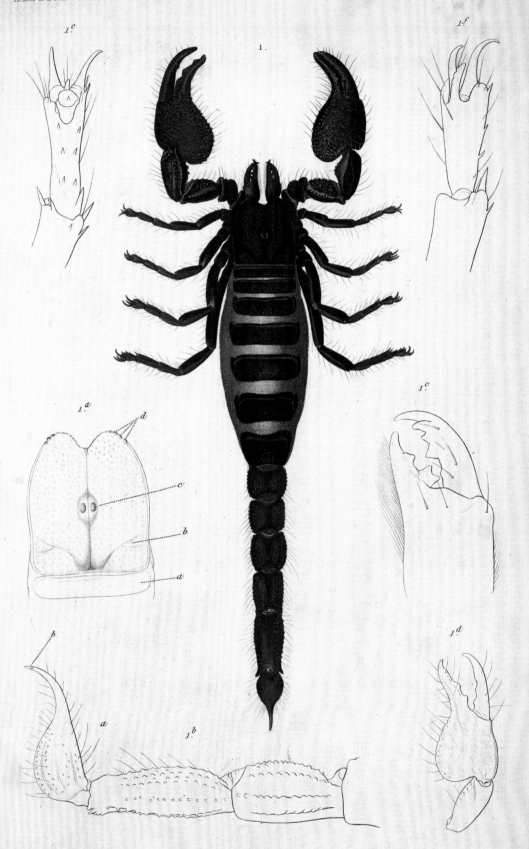

N. Rémond imp.

1. *SCORPION D'AFRIQUE*. (Scorpio Afer.)

The explorer Alexander von Humboldt sent two
axolotl specimens preserved in alcohol to Georges
Cuvier at the beginning of the nineteenth century.
Cuvier assumed that they were larval examples of
an as-yet-unknown reptile. However, in 1865, six live
specimens at the Musée d'Histoire Naturelle in Paris
were observed to breed, revealing their anomalous
ability to reproduce in their tadpole form.

An invented creature(?).
From an 'Album of drawings
by Catesby, G. Edwards, G. Jago et al.,'
eighteenth century.

The album from which this image comes contains a selection
of otherwise apparently realistic and accurate drawings and
paintings of fish and aquatic creatures (including one where
a dried specimen of the fish is pasted beside the drawing).
This clearly invented creature seems to be an anomaly.

PLATE III.

Peter Smit del. et lith.   Mintern Bros. Chromo.

Group of animals exhibiting warning coloration.

'*Group of animals exhibiting warning coloration*'.
Frank Evers Beddard, *Animal Coloration*, London, 1892

Beddard's book was a response to another, recent book on the same topic, but took a less strongly Darwinian line. Beddard thought that there were other factors at work in the development of animals' coloration besides natural selection. He examined the possibility that certain protective chemicals happened to produce bright colours, as opposed to the Darwinian explanation that bright coloration was independently inherited and selected as a protective 'warning'.

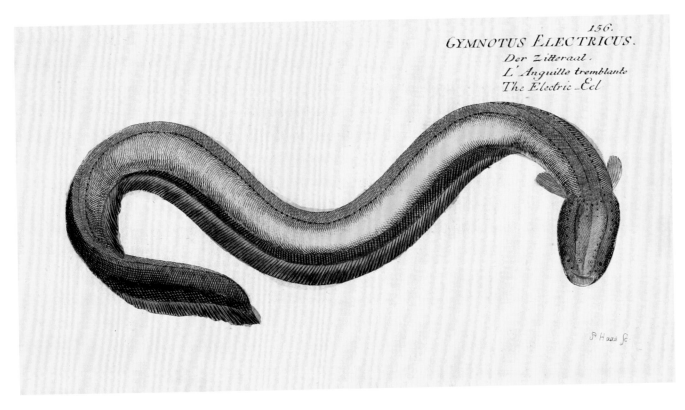

Electric eel ('*Gymnotus electricus*').
Marcus Elieser Bloch,
Naturgeschichte der ausländische Fische,
Berlin, 1786–7

The electric eel was a contested animal in a deep
philosophical argument of the late eighteenth century
about the relationship between electricity and the
body. Was it an anomalous property of the eel, or was
it – as Galvani's frog experiments might indicate –
inherent to animals of all kinds? If the latter,
it suggested that electricity, and not the soul,
was the source of human life itself.

'Cloth worm or larvae of the cloths moth,
wand'ring mite, and crab-like insect'.
Robert Hooke, *Micrographia restaurata*,
London, 1745

Hooke observed several of these mites (left of picture)
wandering across his windowpane during the autumn of 1661.
Examining them, he concluded that he might have found the
answer to a long-standing scientific paradox: the seemingly
spontaneous generation of mites in cheese, flour, leather, and
the like. Although they did not look the same as the vermin
in question, he suspected that the types of insect under his
microscope might well be their progenitors.

'The great-bellyed, or female Gnat'.
Robert Hooke,
Micrographia Restaurata,
London, 1745

Hooke observed the gnat's metamorphosis. 'It drew out its legs
[from its former body], first the two formost, then the other, at
length its whole body perfect and entire appear'd out of the
husk … and by degrees it began to move, and after flew about
the Glass a perfect Gnat.' Hooke was pleased with his discovery:
'I have not found that any Authour has observ'd the like, and
because the thing it self is so strange and heterogeneous from
the usual progress of other Animals, that I judge it may not
onely be pleasant, but very usefull and necessary towards the
compleating of Natural History.'

Louse.
Robert Hooke,
Micrographia,
London, 1665

Hooke's contemporary,
the Dutch microscopist
and naturalist Jan
Swammerdam, prefaced
his own dissection of
this creature with the
memorable announcement:
'Herewith I offer you the
Omnipotent Finger of God
in the anatomy of a louse.'
Hooke seems altogether
more down to earth about
the creature, and about the
creator, whom he designates
merely as 'Nature' and refers
to as though he or she is a
mechanical inventor much
like Hooke himself.

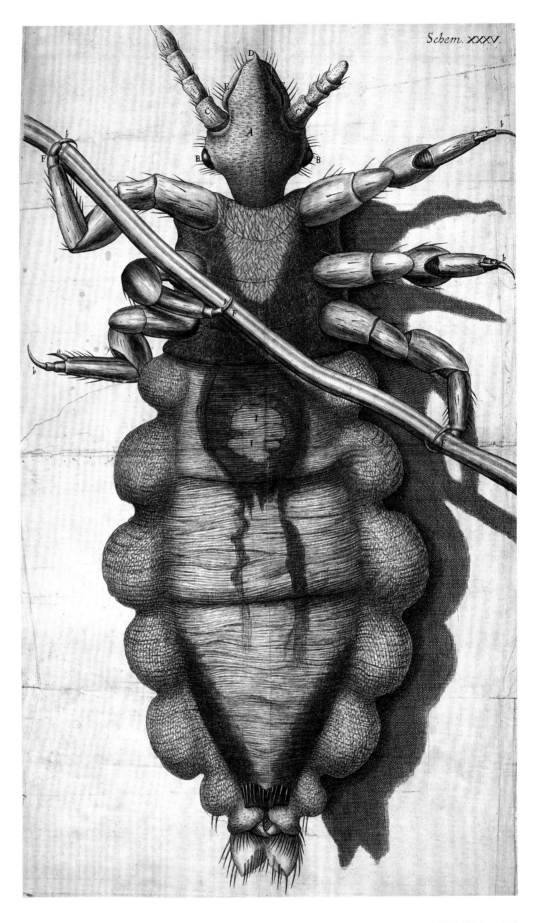

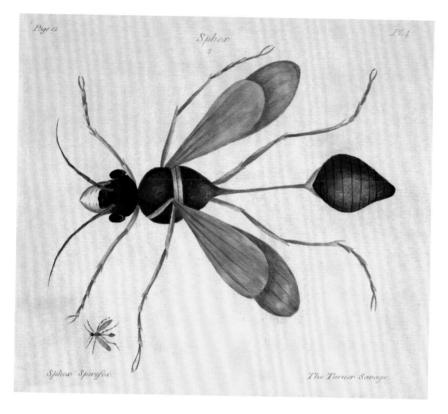

Ichneumon wasp ('*Sphex Spirafex,
The Turner Savage*').

'*Tenthredo Variegata, Mottled Saw-fly*'.
Both from John Hill,
*Insects in their Natural Size; and as
They Appear before the Microscope:
Drawn and Engraved from Nature*,
London, 1772

The sawfly is often parasitised by
ichneumon wasps. Turner notes that
the Sphex is 'the fiercest of all Flys;
they will attack Insects much larger
than themselves'. The Turner Savage
is perhaps the most appalling of these
wasps: 'it is beyond measure terrible to
the lesser insects … there is a part of its
history strangely replete with horror: …
this creature lays her eggs in the body
of a living Caterpillar: they hatch, and
eat that creature up, even while itself
is feeding: at their appointed time they
hatch: and twas long a wonder among
the curious, how a Caterpillar produced
this Fly, instead of a Butterfly, or Moth;
or how one Insect changed to many.'

Ichneumon wasps
('*Genus IV. Ichneumones. Genus V.
Spheges. Genus VI. Chrysis*').
James Barbut,
*Les genres des insectes de Linné;
constatés par divers échantillons
d'insectes d'Angleterre, copiés d'après
nature* ('The Genera Insectorum of
Linnaeus Exemplified in Various
Speciments of English Insects
Drawn from Nature').
Text in English and French. London, 1781

The naturalist Dru Drury remarked on the
beneficial effects of the ichneumon in
his *Illustrations of Natural History* (1770);
by laying its eggs in other insects and so
destroying them, it preserved the 'just
equilibrium' in which human crops could
flourish. Drury was moved to cry: 'When I
say, we behold this, the mind can scarcely
forbear crying out, under a rapturous
sense of conviction, "every thing is good"'.

GENUS IV. *Ichneumones.*

GENUS V. *Spheges.*

GENUS VI. *Chrysis.*

Jaᵉ. *Barbut delin.*

Jaᵉ. *Newton sculp.*

Publiſh'd as the Act directs Febʸ.9.1780, by Jᵉ.Barbut.Nº.101 Strand.

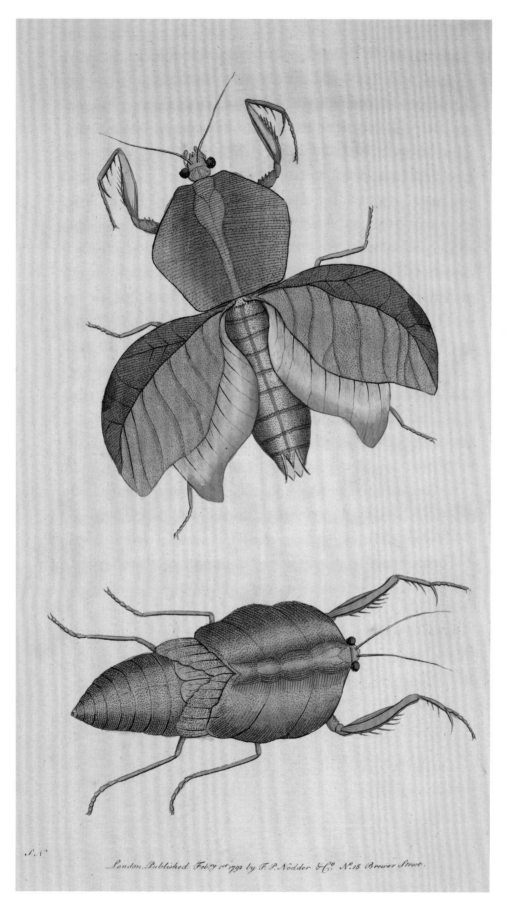

'*Mantis strumaria. Leaf mantis. A type of praying mantis native to South America*'.
George Shaw,
The Naturalist's Miscellany,
London, 1789–1813

The marvellous devices by which insects concealed themselves from their hunters (here, disguising themselves as leaves) were, for the natural theologian, a clear instance of God's careful creativity. Later in the nineteenth century – most particularly for the naturalist Charles Kingsley – camouflage would come to form a troubling challenge to nature's inherent 'truthfulness'; an unreliable narrator lurking in 'the book of nature'.

London. Published Feb.y 1.st 1792 by F. P. Nodder &C.o N.o 15 Brewer Street.

Giant bush cricket, Sumatra.
Watercolour by Sita Ram, *c.* 1800.
William Marsden Collection

Edward Donovan, in his *Epitome of the Natural History of the Insects of India: and the Islands in the Indian Seas* (1800) may have described this insect as *Locusta amboinensis*, although the head in this picture appears more petite than in Donovan's. Donovan notes: 'the wing-cases, as usual in this tribe, bear no very distant resemblance to the leaves of certain plants, not only in colour but also in the outline, and still more so in the conformation of the nerves which arise and branch off towards the extremities, exactly in the same manner as the nerves arise, and ramify, from the mid-rib in the leaves of the far greater number of plants'.

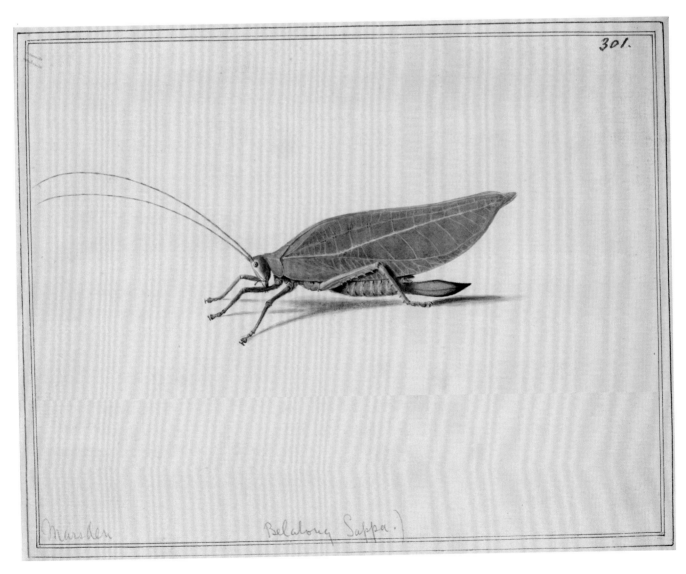

301.

Marsden   Belalong Sappa.)

'The Colorado Potato-Beetle'.
Piece of ephemera,
London, date unknown

This alarmingly magnified beetle serves as (arguably legitimate) propaganda against the spreading Colorado beetle. The beetle began its disastrously effective consumption of potatoes in the nineteenth century, after the crop was introduced to the United States, causing international consternation.

OPPOSITE
Two-headed snake.
George Edwards,
A Natural History of Uncommon Birds, and of Some Other Rare and Undescribed Animals,
London, 1743–51

'I did not propose at first in this Natural History to exhibit Monsters,' Edwards explained. To do so would not have been unusual; copies of Linnaeus' *Systema naturae* from this period still included them. But somehow Edwards did not feel that monsters were quite the thing for a natural history ... except ... they were just so *interesting*.

THE COLORADO POTATO-BEETLE
(DORYPHORA DECEMLINEATA)
HIGHLY MAGNIFIED.

E.C.R.

NATURAL SIZE.

PRICE 6ᴰ HARDWICKE & BOGUE, 192 PICCADILLY, LONDON, W.

ABOVE
Flying squirrel.
Original drawing by Jacobus Theodorus Klein, from 'Descriptive notes, letters etc. to Sir Hans Sloane with coloured drawings of natural history', (manuscript), 1726–40

Klein was a European cosmopolitan and polymath. His illustrations (if they are his) cover the gamut from lifelike presentation, via representative flying posture, through to anatomy.

LEFT
Flying squirrel.
Arnout Vosmaer,
Description d'un recueil exquis d'animaux rares, consistent en quadrupèdes, oiseaux et serpents, des Indes Orientales et Occidentales, s'ayant trouvés ci-devant vivants aux Ménageries appartenantes à Monseigneur le Prince d'Orange-Nassau, Amsterdam, 1804

The various species of flying squirrel are widely distributed around the globe, though they are descended from a single evolutionary ancestor. The first European description appears to be on Willem Blaeu's annotated map of the far northern American continent in 1534.

Flying lizard.
From George Edwards, E. Kirkius et al.,
'Amphibians and Reptiles',
(manuscript collection), first half
of the eighteenth century

Luigi Bossi included the flying lizard *Draco volans*
in his *Dei basilischi, dragoni ed altri animali creduti
favolosi* ('Basilisks, Dragons and other Animals
Believed Fabulous') in 1792. The animal had been
listed by Linnaeus, and not amongst
the paradoxical ones.

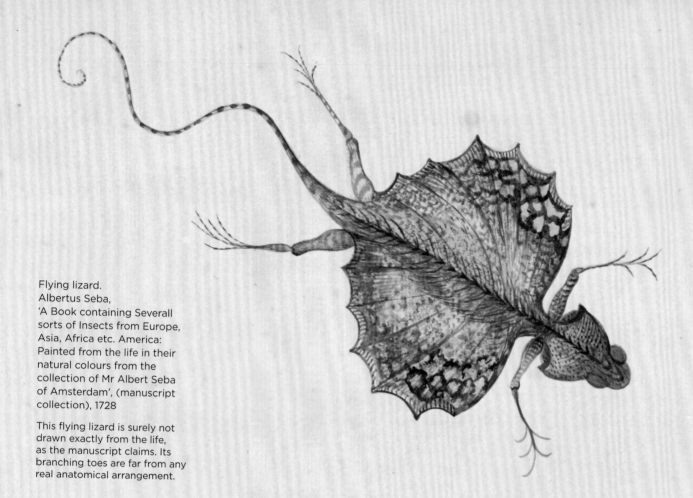

Flying lizard.
Albertus Seba,
'A Book containing Severall
sorts of Insects from Europe,
Asia, Africa etc. America:
Painted from the life in their
natural colours from the
collection of Mr Albert Seba
of Amsterdam', (manuscript
collection), 1728

This flying lizard is surely not
drawn exactly from the life,
as the manuscript claims. Its
branching toes are far from any
real anatomical arrangement.

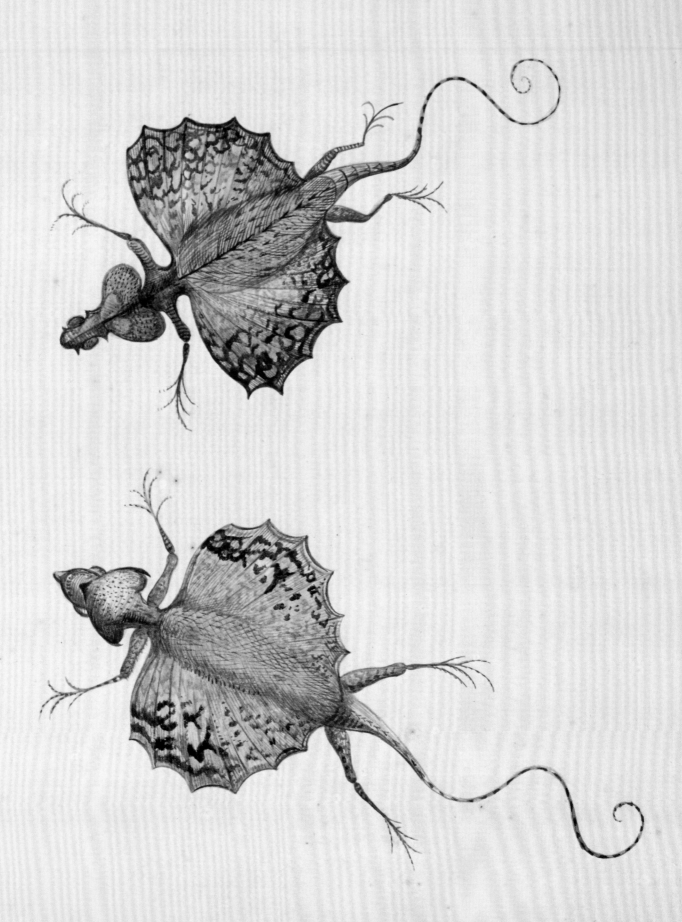

The anomalous nature of flightless birds has been long accommodated into systems of knowledge. Pliny the Elder made the ostrich his very first specimen in his chapter on birds, but noted that although 'wings have been given to aid it in running; in other respects ostriches cannot be considered as birds, and do not raise themselves from the earth'. Indeed, he thought, they almost approached 'to the nature of quadrupeds'.

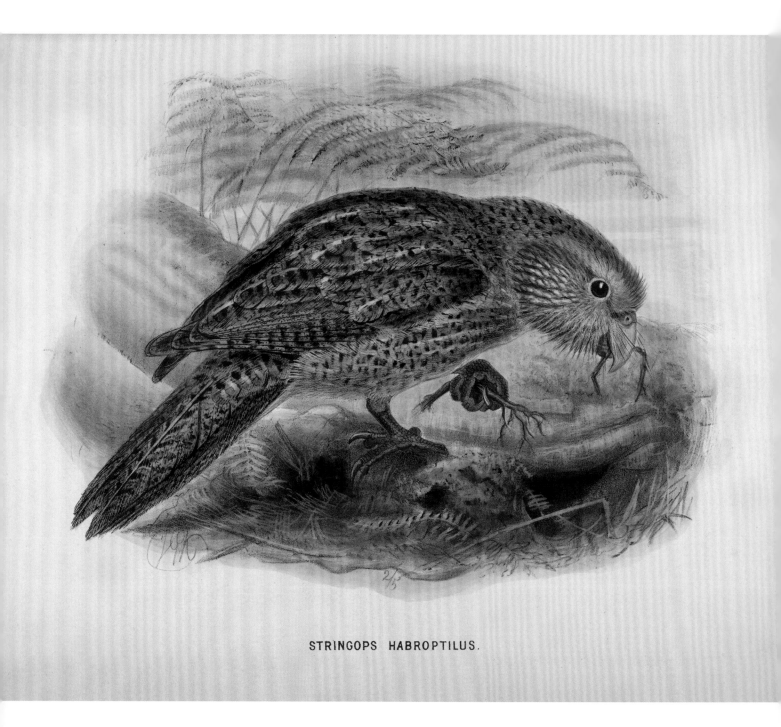

STRINGOPS HABROPTILUS.

This Bird is

feet — Inch

from foot to the back — 3 — 2½

from back to the tail — 3 — 5

from back to the Bill — 1 — 10½

This bird eat some Goafnuits & 100 Plantain fruit
Quarter measure rice boiled with the milk in a Day
He likewise swallow Garlicks, Onions & small stones
which stones comes out with his dung in the same manner

She has laid an Egg after it came to My Palace
which the size & colour of the egg is just like
Pumplamas fruite

Mysore Ellection
of Drawings

Cross between a donkey and a zebra
('*Métis femelle d'Ane et de Zebre*').
Étienne Geoffroy Saint-Hilaire,
Histoire naturelle des mammifères,
Paris, 1824–42

This apparently innocent zebroid, as zebra crosses are now known, belies a complex history of transgression. Zebroids were produced in the course of equine husbandry, in efforts to improve the stock, but became embroiled in arguments about inheritance that reached into questions of race and aristocracy. Queen Charlotte's zebra was unkindly christened 'the Queen's ass' as debates about inherited superiority collided with an unloved monarch.

Métis femelle d'Ane et de Zébre.

Mongoose.
(*The Ichneumon,
Viverra ichneumon*).
George Shaw,
*Musei Leveriani explicatio,
Anglica et Latina (containing
select specimens from the
museum of the late Sir
Ashton Lever, Kt., with
descriptions in Latin and
English)*, London, 1792

The mongoose, perhaps
surprisingly, shares its name
'ichneumon' with the wasps
on pages 232 and 233. This
name, in the ancient world,
designated creatures who
served a useful function
in relation to humankind.
The wasps parasitically
predated upon insect
pests that might otherwise
damage eighteenth-century
farmers' crops; the weasel,
traditionally, was well known
for stealing crocodile eggs
and killing asps – thus
doing service to the ancient
Egyptians. As any reader
of Kipling knows, the
mongoose killed cobras
lurking in the Indian homes
of British colonists.

THE BLACK RAT.

'*The Black Rat*'.
William MacGillivray,
A History of British Quadrupeds,
Vol. 13 in Jardine's
The Naturalist's Library,
London, 1843

The black rat was already in decline in Britain by
the time this picture was made, being replaced by
the larger brown rat. There is a level of ambiguity
to the image: the rats' eyes interrogate the viewer,
demanding our opinion about the trap that is
about to spring shut on them. And those rats in
the background, amongst the bucolic hay: are they
playing or fleeing? Or performing dives into death?

The dinosaurs displayed at the Crystal Palace ('*Extinct Animals*'). Matthew Digby Wyatt, *Views of the Crystal Palace and Park, Sydenham*, London, 1854

The great fossil discoveries of the eighteenth and nineteenth centuries were almost immediately paradoxical, especially in relation to Noah's Ark, which now had to be expanded in imagination to accommodate the new finds. Alternatively, as some geologists speculated, the Flood could be invoked as explanation for the death and disappearance of these puzzling animal-kinds.

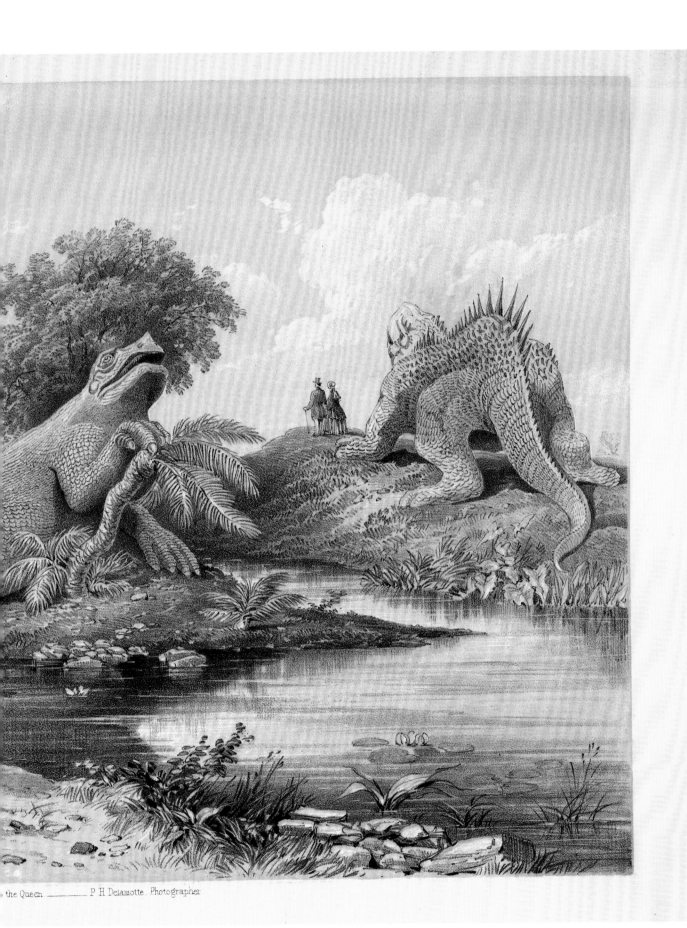

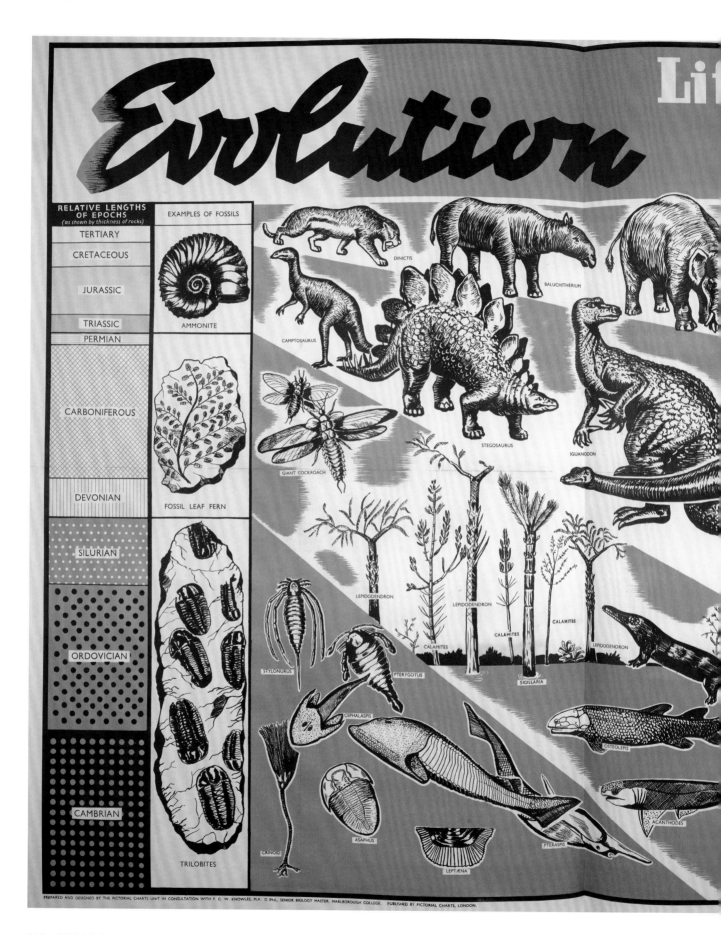

'*Evolution: Life in the Past*'.
School poster, early twentieth century

This poster, refreshingly, gives visual
credit to Charles Lyell for the concept of
evolution – as did Charles Darwin himself:
'I always feel as if my books came half out
of Lyell's brain.' Lyell indeed expanded
the span of geological history in the
nineteenth-century imagination to a
scale allowing time for evolution by the
accumulation of tiny variations to occur.
He was, however, initially a friendly critic
of 'natural selection', fearing that the
concept effectively deified nature.

BELOW LEFT
'A Domesticated Female Orang Outang'.

BELOW RIGHT
*'The Orang Outang or Wild Man
of the Woods'.*

OPPOSITE
*'Representation of the Analogy
betwixt Man & Brute'.*
All from Ebenezer Sibly,
*An Universal System of Natural History
Including the Natural History of Man, Etc.*,
London, 1794–1807

Of all the great apes, orang-utans sit most exactly on the borderline of historical debates about distinctions between humans and animals. Edward Tyson, in *Orang-Outang, sive Homo Sylvestris: or, the Anatomy of a Pygmie Compared with that of a Monkey, an Ape, and a Man* (1699) found a number of differences but even more similarities between human and ape (actually a chimpanzee). The eighteenth-century philosopher James Burnett, Lord Monboddo, claimed: 'I believe it will be very difficult, or rather, impossible, for a man, who is accustomed to divide things according to specific marks, not individual differences, to draw the line betwixt the Orang Outang and the dumb persons among us.' These apparent difficulties, far predating the monkey politics of Darwinian evolution, tended to inspire prurient and demeaning comparisons between the animal and persons of doubtful human status, namely slaves and women (or, best of all, a combination of the two).

A Domesticated Female, Orang Outang.

Published as the Act directs, June 25, 1795.

The Orang-Outang, or Wild Man of the Woods.

Published as the Act directs, June 1, 1795.

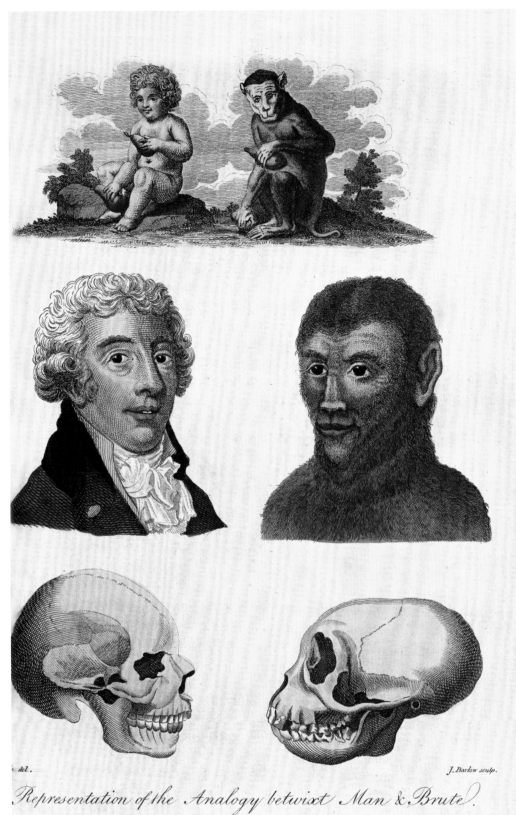

Representation of the Analogy betwixt Man & Brute.

Published as the Act directs, Jan. 16. 1796.

J. Barlow sculp.

NOTES

1 Paula Findlen, *Possessing Nature: Museums, Collecting, and Scientific Culture in Early Modern Italy* (University of California Press, 1996), 91.

2 Francis Haskell and Henrietta McBurney, 'The paper museum of Cassiano dal Pozzo', *Visual Resources* 14.1 (1998), 1–17.

3 Aldrovandi quoted in Findlen, *Possessing Nature*, 69.

4 Quoted in Umberto Eco, *The Aesthetics of Thomas Aquinas* (Cambridge, MA: Harvard University Press, 1988), 9.

5 Hermann Walter, 'An illustrated incunable of Pliny's Natural History in the Biblioteca Palatina, Parma', *Journal of the Warburg and Courtauld Institutes* (1990), 208–16.

6 Jeffrey Ashcroft, 'Art in German: Artistic statements by Albrecht Dürer', *Forum for Modern Language Studies*, 48.4 (2012), 376–88; at 386.

7 Claudia Swan, *Art, Science, and Witchcraft in Early Modern Holland: Jacques de Gheyn II (1565–1629)* (Cambridge: Cambridge University Press, 2005), 10–11.

8 Sachiko Kusukawa, *Picturing the Book of Nature: Image, Text, and Argument in Sixteenth-Century Human Anatomy and Medical Botany* (Chicago: University of Chicago Press, 2012), 37–40.

9 Natalie Lawrence, 'Assembling the dodo in early modern natural history', *The British Journal for the History of Science*, 48.3 (2015), 387–408; at 405.

10 Laurent Pinon, 'Conrad Gessner and the historical depth of Renaissance natural history'. In G. Pomata and N. G. Siraisi (eds), *Historia: Empiricism and Erudition in Early Modern Europe* (Cambridge, MA: The MIT Press, 2005), 241–67.

11 Sachiko Kusukawa, 'The sources of Gessner's pictures for the *Historia animalium*', *Annals of Science* 67.3 (2010), 303–28; Kusukawa's free translation at 307.

12 Kusukawa, *Picturing the Book of Nature*, 175.

13 Cynthia M. Pyle, 'Art as science: Scientific illustration, 1490–1670 in drawing, woodcut and copper plate', *Endeavour* 24.2 (2000), 69–75; at 74.

14 Kusukawa, 'The sources of Gessner's pictures'; see also Laurent Pinon in Pomata and Siraisi (eds), *Historia: Empiricism and Erudition* at 254.

15 Lorraine Daston and Peter Galison, *Objectivity* (New York: Zone Books, 2008), 42 and 66.

16 David Freedberg, *The Eye of the Lynx: Galileo, his Friends, and the Beginnings of Modern Natural History* (Chicago: University of Chicago Press, 2003), 57.

17 Robert Hooke, *Micrographia, or, Some Physiological Descriptions of Minute Bodies Made By Magnifying Glasses:With Observations and Inquiries Thereupon* (London : Jo. Martyn and Ja. Allestry, printers to the Royal Society, 1665), unpaginated [page 2 of 'Preface'].

18 Matthew C. Hunter, *Wicked Intelligence: Visual Art and the Science of Experiment in Restoration London* (Chicago: University of Chicago Press, 2013), 133.

19 Pyle, 'Art as science', 69–75.

20 Clark Art Institute, *Inside Albrecht's Studio – Engraving*. https://www.youtube.com/watch?v=Qf4sH8iCOPw [accessed 1 March 2016].

21 George Edwards, quoted in Victoria Dickenson, *Drawn from Life: Science and Art in the Portrayal of the New World* (Toronto: University of Toronto Press, 1998), 160–1.

22 Claudia Swan, *Art, Science, and Witchcraft in Early Modern Holland: Jacques de Gheyn II (1565–1629)* (Cambridge: Cambridge University Press, 2005), 41.

23 David R. Brigham, 'Mark Catesby and the patronage of natural history in the first half of the eighteenth century'. In A. Meyers and M. Pritchard (eds), *Empire's Nature: Mark Catesby's New World Vision* (Chapel Hill: UNC Press, 1998), 91–146.

24 Dickenson, *Drawn from Life*, 150.

25 Joyce E. Chaplin, 'Mark Catesby, a skeptical Newtonian in America'. In Meyers and Pritchard (eds), *Empire's Nature*, 34–90.

26 Theodore E. Stebbins, Jr, 'Audubon's drawings of American birds, 1805–38'. In A. Blaugrund and T. Stebbins, Jr (eds), *John James Audubon: The Watercolours for* The Birds of America (New York: The New York Historical Society, 1993), 3–26.

27 David Elliston Allen, *Books and Naturalists* (London: Collins, 2010), 165.

28 Allen, *Books and Naturalists*, 248 and 325.

29 Charlotte Sleigh, 'Jan Swammerdam's frogs', *Notes and Records of the Royal Society*, 66.4 (2012), 373–92.

30 Allen, *Books and Naturalists*, 27–8.

31 Warren D. Allmon, 'The evolution of accuracy in natural history illustration: Reversal of printed illustrations of snails and crabs in pre-Linnaean works suggests indifference to morphological detail', *Archives of Natural History* 34.1 (2007), 174–91.

32 Anna Marie Roos, *Web of Nature: Martin Lister (1639–1712), the First Arachnologist* (Leiden: Brill, 2011).

33 Sachiko Kusukawa, 'The Historia Piscium (1686)', *Notes and Records of the Royal Society* 54.2 (2000), 179–97.

34 Kusukawa, 'The Historia Piscium', 186.

35 Allen, *Books and Naturalists*, 171.

36 Allen, *Books and Naturalists*, 267.

37 Allen, *Books and Naturalists*, 227.

38 Colonel R[ichard] Meinertzhagen, *Kenya Diary: 1902–1907* (Edinburgh: Oliver and Boyd, 1957), 2.

39 Meinertzhagen, *Diary*, 7.

40 Daston and Galison, *Objectivity*; George Levine, *Dying to Know: Scientific Epistemology and Narrative in Victorian England* (Chicago: University of Chicago Press, 2002).

41 Meinertzhagen, *Diary*, 17.

42 *Observer*, 4 October 2015. *The New Review* pp. 22–23; p. 22. See Craig Packer, *Lions in the Balance: Man-Eaters, Manes and Men with Guns* (Chicago: University of Chicago Press, 2015).

43 Charles St John, *Natural History & Sport in Moray* (Edinburgh: Edmonston and Douglas, 1863), 137.

44 Emily Crofford, *Gone Forever: The Great Auk* (New York: Crestwood House, 1989), 43.

45 John M. MacKenzie, *The Empire of Nature: Hunting, Conservation and British Imperialism* (Manchester: Manchester University Press, 1997).

46 Meinertzhagen, *Diary*, 14.

47 J. F. M. Clark, 'Morris, Francis Orpen (1810–1893)', *Oxford Dictionary of National Biography*, (Oxford: Oxford University Press, 2004) http://www.oxforddnb.com/view/article/19304 [accessed 3 Nov 2015].

48 Allen, *Books and Naturalists*, 327.

49 Helen Macdonald, *H is For Hawk* (London: Jonathan Cape, 2014), 181.

50 Allen, *Books and Naturalists*, 195–7.

51 David Allen, 'Tastes and crazes'. In N. Jardine, J. Secord, and E. Spary (eds), *Cultures of Natural History* (Cambridge: Cambridge University Press, 1996), 394–407.

52 Francis Haskell and Henrietta McBurney, 'The paper museum of Cassiano dal Pozzo', *Visual Resources* 14.1 (1998), 1–17.

AUTHOR'S NOTE   FURTHER READING

I am indebted to the scholarship of the following authors for information included in the captions: T. R. Birkhead et al., Miguel Carneiro et al., Elio Corti & Fernando Civardi, Sarah Franklin, Miranda Kadwell et al., Sachiko Kusukawa, Ben Marsh, G. F. Mees, Janice Neri, Mary Orr, Janis L. Pallister, Christopher Plumb, Kristopher Poole, Christian Reiß et al., Janine Rogers, Sheila Wille. *The Oxford Dictionary of National Biography* was also an invaluable source.

Allen, David Elliston, *Books and Naturalists* (London: Collins, 2010)

Allen, David Elliston, *The Naturalist in Britain: A Social History* (Princeton: Princeton University Press, 1976)

Daston, Lorraine and Peter Galison, *Objectivity* (New York: Zone Books, 2008)

Dickenson, Victoria, *Drawn from Life: Science and Art in the Portrayal of the New World* (Toronto: University of Toronto Press, 1998)

Findlen, Paula, *Possessing Nature: Museums, Collecting, and Scientific Culture in Early Modern Italy* (Oakland, CA: University of California Press, 1994)

Freedberg, David, *The Eye of the Lynx: Galileo, his Friends, and the Beginnings of Modern Natural History* (Chicago: University of Chicago Press, 2003)

Hunter, Matthew C., *Wicked Intelligence: Visual Art and the Science of Experiment in Restoration London* (Chicago: University of Chicago Press, 2013)

Kusukawa, Sachiko, *Picturing the Book of Nature: Image, Text, and Argument in Sixteenth-Century Human Anatomy and Medical Botany* (Chicago: University of Chicago Press, 2012)

MacKenzie, John M., *The Empire of Nature: Hunting, Conservation and British Imperialism* (Manchester: Manchester University Press, 1997)

Meyers, Amy R. W. and Margaret Beck Pritchard, eds, *Empire's Nature: Mark Catesby's New World Vision* (Chapel Hill: University of North Carolina Press, 1998)

Neri, Janice, *The Insect and the Image: Visualizing Nature in Early Modern Europe, 1500-1700* (Minneapolis: University of Minnesota Press, 2011)

Plumb, Christopher, *The Georgian Menagerie: Exotic Animals in Eighteenth-Century London* (London: IB Tauris, 2015)

Pyle, Cynthia M., 'Art as science: Scientific illustration, 1490–1670 in drawing, woodcut and copper plate', *Endeavour* 24.2 (2000), 69–75

Ritvo, Harriet, *The Animal Estate: The English and Other Creatures in the Victorian Age* (Cambridge, MA: Harvard University Press, 1987)

Ritvo, Harriet, *Noble Cows and Hybrid Zebras: Essays on Animals and History* (Charlottesville: University of Virginia Press, 2010)

Ritvo, Harriet, *The Platypus and the Mermaid, and Other Figments of the Classifying Imagination* (Cambridge, MA: Harvard University Press, 1997)

Rogers, Janine, *Eagle* (London: Reaktion, 2015)

Roos, Anna Marie, *Web of Nature: Martin Lister (1639–1712), the First Arachnologist* (Leiden: Brill, 2011)

Sleigh, Charlotte, *Frog* (London: Reaktion, 2012)

Swan, Claudia, *Art, Science, and Witchcraft in Early Modern Holland: Jacques de Gheyn II (1565–1629)* (Cambridge: Cambridge University Press, 2005)

Wille, Sheila, 'The ichneumon fly and the equilibration of British natural economies in the eighteenth century', *The British Journal for the History of Science* 48.4 (2015), 639–60

INDEX

Numbers in *italics* refer to illustrations and captions within the introductory essays. Latinate names are not usually indexed unless no common name is given in the source material. Names given in the original publications, and quoted in this volume, may have been superseded by modern nomenclature.